The Healing of
FEARS

H. Norman Wright

HARVEST HOUSE PUBLISHERS
Eugene, Oregon 97402

The Healing of Fears

Copyright © 1982 Harvest House Publishers
Eugene, Oregon 97402
Library of Congress Catalog Card Number 81-83238
ISBN 0-89081-302-7

Printed in the United States of America.

CONTENTS

Introduction   5
1. Fears   9
2. Becoming All That God Wants
   You To Become 21
3. Childhood Fears 35
4. Fears and Phobias 47
5. Worry—What Is It? 55
6. Controlling Your Worry 71
7. How To Control Your Thoughts . . . 93
8. Steps In Overcoming Fear 111
9. Facing Your Fear 131
10. The Ultimate Fear 145

INTRODUCTION

"I was afraid—so I hid myself." A familiar phrase? Yes, familiar, but as old as the beginning of mankind, for it was Adam who uttered these words. Right from the start man has attempted to hide. Why? He was afraid then, and he has continued to be afraid right down to the present day. Oh, our life-styles have changed and we are more sophisticated and modern— but our basic fears remain. Fear stalked the human race thousands of years ago and it remains with us now. Who are we afraid of? Who else but other people, ourselves and God! And this fear often directs and controls the very direction of our lives.

You are like the rest of us. At times you experience fear. You worry sometimes. You might even feel anxious, or have a problem you can't seem to get rid of. Whatever you interpret as a threat can elicit fear. If you didn't worry or experience fear you would be abnormal! Fear affects almost everyone. We all vary in what triggers off our fear and worries, but there are certain events which bring a fear response in all of us. A car hurtling at us or a vicious lion about to spring doesn't make us calm! In today's world with runaway prices, inflation, recession, terrorism, increased crime, and marital discord, we have much to be concerned about.

Anxiety is a feeling of dread, apprehension or uneasiness. It produces a sense of approaching danger but does not always come from a reasonable cause. Some people feel uneasy or apprehensive but cannot identify a reason. The source of the impending doom is not clear. Many words in our language are used to indicate variations of anxiety: apprehension, uneasiness, nervousness, worry, disquiet, misgiving, edginess, unnerved, unsettled, upset, aghast, and many more.

Worry and fear are close cousins. When the cause of worry is identifiable, it is usually called fear.

The word fear comes from the Old English word *faer* meaning sudden calamity or danger. The Latin word *anxious* is the basis for anxious and means troubled in mind about some uncertain event. It can also mean a divided mind.

All of us have fears. But how many and how intense are yours?

The fears of today are the same as the fears of yesterday. Many known figures of history were fearful. Robert Burton in his *Anatomy of Melancholy* mentioned that Demosthe suffered from stage fright and Augustus Caesar was unable to sit in the dark.[1] Burton described patients who had the following life story. He would, ''not walk alone from home, for fear he should swoon, or die. A second fears every man he meets will rob him, quarrel with him, or kill him. A third dare not venture to walk alone, for fear he should meet the devil, a thief, be sick . . . another dares not go over a bridge, come near a pool, brook, steep hill, lie in a chamber where cross-beams are, for fear he be tempted to hang, drown or precipitate himself. If he be in a silent auditory, as at a sermon, he is afraid he shall speak aloud, at unawares, something indecent, unfit to be said. If he be locked in a close room, he is afraid of being stifled for want of air, and still carried bisket, aqua-vitae, or some strong waters about him, for fear of deliquiums (fainting), or being sick; or if he be in a throng, middle of a church, multitude, where he may not well get out, though he sit at ease, he is so misaffected.''[2]

But we can learn to overcome these fears in order to live the life God intended us to. We are given a biblical solution to our problems, and we have only but to use it.

—H. Norman Wright

[1]R. Burton, *The Anatomy of Melancholy*, II Th. Ed., London, 1813; first published in 1621.

[2]Ibid. Pg. 27,28.

1
Fears

Our fears cover the gamut of human experience and include fear of exams, spiders, darkness, mice, heights, foreigners, and hundreds of other things. Do you avoid walking under a ladder or feel uneasy if a black cat crosses in front of you? These minor fears are called superstitions.

We show our fear in different ways. Some people experience a sensation internally which is not really observable. Others sweat and their heart pounds. Some people come unglued, scream and run away. Others freeze and cannot move. Habakkuk the prophet experienced the effects of fear which are so common to all of us. "I heard, and my [whole inner self] trembled, my lips quivered at the sound. Rottenness enters into my bones and under me—down to my feet—I tremble" (Habakkuk 3:16 AMP). The physical effects of fear are varied. In addition to sweating and heart pounding the skin can appear pale, hair stands on end, and blood pressure rises. There may be increased blood flowing through the muscles causing greater tension, dryness and tightness of the throat and mouth, an increased need to urinate and defi- cate, butterflies or buzzards flying in your stomach, paralyzing weakness in the arms and legs, difficulty in breathing or a tightness in the chest. Again Scripture gives the same descrip- tion of the results of fear and worry. "Anxiety in a man's heart weighs it down" (Proverbs 12:25 AMP).

There are healthy and unhealthy fears. But do you know the difference? Healthy fears include:

. . . wearing a seat belt in a plane or car to avoid injury.

. . . wearing a life jacket in a canoe on a river trip.

. . . checking out wild berries before eating them by asking an expert.

. . . asking a financial expert for advice before making investments.

Any of these normal concerns and fears could move into the unhealthy stage by never riding in a car, plane, or canoe, never eating any ber- ries, never investing, etc. Severe anxiety or fear hinders a person's performance. It can actually cause paralysis. But what about the benefits of fear or anxiety? Many individuals in various professions have said that a mild degree of fear and anxiety increases their effectiveness. Ac- tors, speakers, politicians, football players, salespeople, runners, and fighter pilots are a few of those individuals who feel they perform bet- ter with a certain amount of anxiety.

In an extreme crisis, however, fear may be so intense that the panic creates even greater trauma. A mother fleeing a fire in a theater may forget to take her child with her. Too much fear brings mistakes. But too little fear can cause carelessness and even a disregard for dangerous situations. Firemen cannot be rash and careless nor can army troops. An interesting study of hospital patients found that those who appeared fearless prior to an operation experienced excessive postoperative pain and discomfort. They demonstrated more anger and resentment than patients who were moderately fearful before their operation. But patients who were highly anxious before their operation were still fearful afterward and complained of discomfort.

What is an excessive fear in your life? Where did it originate? What are the results? When do you experience productive fear or anxiety?

We were not created to live in a continual state of apprehension. Our lives are not to be a reflection of timidity and fear. You may want deliverance from fear, but not all of your fears. Fear is the fuel which moves you out of a dangerous situation. Positive fear can save your life. But fear which gnaws at your life and disrupts your sense of calmness is what we seek to eliminate. Much of our fear is directed toward possible eventualities and here is where our fear blends into worry.

A heart attack, the stock market collapsing, war between Russia and the U.S., and the end of the world are all things which cannot be prevented by fearing them. The energy which we expend in fear and worry can keep us in a state of anxiety as it builds and swells within us. We end up being too afraid to live life!

There is one type of fear we need. In fact, having this fear can lead to the eradication of other fears in our lives. It can bring a positive response to life. It is the fear of God. Webster defines this kind of fear as "awe, profound reverence, especially for the Supreme Being." The word reverence means "veneration; honor; respect; act of obedience."

Over and over again Scripture talks of the fear of the Lord.

Job 1:1 "There was a man in the land of Uz, whose name was Job; and that man was perfect and upright, and one that feared God, and eschewed evil."

Job 28:28 "And unto man he said, Behold, the fear of the Lord, that *is* wisdom; and to depart from evil *is* understanding."

Prov. 10:27 "The fear of the Lord prolongeth days: but the years of the wicked shall be shortened."

Prov. 15:16 "Better is little with the fear of the Lord than great treasure and trouble therewith."

Prov. 19:23 "The fear of the Lord *tendeth* to life: and *he that hath it* shall abide satisfied; he shall not be visited with evil."

Prov. 9:10 "The fear of the Lord *is* the beginning of wisdom: and the knowledge of the holy *is* understanding."

Prov. 14:17 "The fear of the Lord *is* a fountain of life, to depart from the snares of death."

Fearing God means to revere Him. It is a

healthy life response.

But what do you fear most? Falling off a thousand foot cliff? Being injured in a Trans-Am race? Being attacked and gored by a raging bull? Probably not. Unusual situations such as these are not usually what frighten us. It is more the everyday events and people who threaten us to such an extent that our life is limited.

Whatever it is that you fear most, do you think you are the only one who feels that way? Think about yourself as your read about two common fears.

Fear of rejection. Many people are afraid of socializing with others, especially strangers. They might be able to perform great feats and acts of courage, but cringe when it comes to reaching out to people. Their fear of others cries out until other people become aware of their discomfort. They may just decide to leave the person alone and then he is left with the feeling of being rejected. Fear of reaching out to others and fear of being rejected go hand in hand. Another way to experience rejection is to avoid socializing and become a recluse. This too brings feelings of rejection and loneliness. Fear is like that—it involves two kinds of pain. One pain comes from doing what you are afraid of and the other comes from avoiding what you are afraid of. Either way pain exists. What most of us do not realize, however, is that in the long run the pain of doing something we are afraid of is less than the pain of avoiding it.

Fear of failure. Fearful people are often perfectionists. Their security comes from doing things better than anyone else. They either drive themselves and other people up a wall in their quest for perfection or they listen to their fear and retreat. They fear ridicule from others and their own inner voices when they are not perfect.

Let's enter the world of the perfectionist for a moment. What is this person like? What makes him or her tick? A perfectionist usually knows he is one. He goes to great lengths to achieve perfection for himself and may also expect it of others. Work and fun are pursued very methodically. He gives great attention to details above and beyond the call of duty. A perfectionist expends more effort than others and yet he feels no real satisfaction. In a sense he is a successful failure, continually striving to do better. He is never satisfied with himself or others. Interruptions, disruptions, changes, irregularities, delays, and surprises are a perfectionist's enemies. His theme song is strive, strive, strive —an endless treadmill.

There are times though when a perfectionist deals with his fear by retreating rather than striving. He withdraws and hesitates because the pain of failure is too much. By not trying he can always say to himself, "I can do it if I try," or "I know I could really do it if I wanted to . . . or had the time," etc. But if he tries he would lose that hope. Withdrawal becomes a protective cocoon. He feels it is less painful than the pain of failure. It is easier to think "I know I can make that speech" than to get up and flub it. A man who fears impotency avoids sex and makes excuses. The pain of failure is too great. And the more he gives in to his fears the greater they become.

The unreasonable demands of the perfectionist placate his need to please himself or others or to feel adequate and eliminate the fear of failure. But whatever is driving him has an insatiable appetite. If you are a perfectionist, what or who are you afraid of? We can never achieve perfection in this life. We can become adequate and out of this adequacy do the best we can. Our adequacy comes from a declaration from God Himself who has declared us to be adequate people. He did this through His Son, Jesus, and His work on the cross. Think about it.

For some reason the two major fears we struggle with are the fear of failure and the fear of rejection. We have all felt these two fears at one time or another. Unfortunately, some people experience them continuously. Rejection is feeling unaccepted by yourself, other people or both. Somewhere in your lifetime you may have been treated as an unacceptable person. Someone, even a parent, may have seen you as a burden. If you were rejected as a child you may either retreat from others or, out of your fear of rejection, seek approval so intense that you push others away.

You may feel a desperate need for affection and approval, but when love is offered you reject it because you question its sincerity. A rejected person short circuits any acceptance that is offered to him. Thus his fear intensifies. What is so strange is the fact that rejected, fearful people tend to seek out other people who reject them. It becomes a vicious circle and appears hopeless when you are caught in the middle of it.

One of the greatest ironies of life is the fact

that one of our greatest fears is the fear of people. Imagine—one person fearing another person—people fearing people. This fear comes in various shapes and sizes. Inferiority, shyness, and timidity reflect this fear. Sometimes these fears become extreme and move into agoraphobia.

How do our fears develop? They grow out of experience or situations in our childhood. It may have been modeled for us by our parents and in some way we pattern our life after them. In many cases our interactions with significant people as a child form our response to others and to ourselves. As a child which of the following did you experience from your parents?

Rejection   Belittling
Hurt   Yelling
Punishment   Non-listening
Impatience   Blame

Our response to such experiences may take such forms as withdrawal, feelings of inferiority, aggression, anger, criticalness. Every hurtful experience you and I suffer leaves some emotional scar tissue. These scars are like ghosts of the past which continue through life with us like uninvited guests. And our fear of people continues to develop even into the marital relationship.

How much of what you do is motivated by fear? Do you know? Have you ever thought about how your life may be dominated by fear? Think about these statements and see if they apply to your own life:

—Fear of what others think about us keeps us from being friendly or speaking up in class.

—Fear of others getting more than us or a better position causes us to act impulsively, to try to beat them, or to devalue them by gossip.

—Fear of being controlled by others or having to conform causes us to dominate others.

—Fear of sharing our weaknesses and inadequacies causes us to act like the strong, silent type.

—Fear of failure keeps us in a life of mediocrity and boredom.

—Fear of financial ruin either keeps us from wise investments and makes us dull and boring by our careful restrictive life-style.

—Fear of God makes us distort who He really is.

And the fears go on and on. What is your fear? What does it cause you to do?

We are told that many people are afraid of death. But I see more people who are afraid of life. Living life to its full potential is a threat to them. Many people experience a personal emotional paralysis. I think we experience some of the pains, hurts and aches of life more vividly than the fear of death. But fear of living creates a present-day death for us. It is actually more fatal than the fear of death. We become the living dead. We hide and insulate ourselves throughout our lifetime and then when death comes, we have thrown away our opportunity to live life.

How strange to choose such a path to follow, especially when Christ came to set the captives free. We have freedom in Christ but yet we choose to put the chains and shackles back on and imprison ourselves in a walking cell.

The fear of living is the fear of being hurt, of being rejected. We make up our minds never to be vulnerable and before long we become an ingrown turtle. The turtle only goes forward or makes progress when he sticks his neck out. Death will come soon enough. Why bring it to pass any sooner? The pain of the living dead is constant and there is no finality. We can be afraid . . . but not immobile. We can be scared . . . but not abound in fear.

Have you ever been in a room that has an echo in it or on a mountain range where your words bounce from peak to peak? In the room or the mountain range your words are repeated. You yell out "Hello" and wait. You hear "Hello" . . . "Hello" . . . "Hello"." Hear the words of Jesus echoing throughout the New Testament and into our daily lives, "Fear not . . . fear not . . . fear not . . . fear not."

We are never, never alone. We do not reach out by ourselves whether it be to another person or a group or a new venture in life. He is with us. He does not isolate us from the hard times of life but plunges through them with us.

Have you not known? Have you not heard? The everlasting God, the Lord, the Creator of the ends of the earth, does not faint or grow weary; there is no searching of His understanding. He gives power to the faint *and* weary, and to him who has no might He increases strength—causing it to multiply and making it abound.

(Isaiah 40:28-29 AMP)

Fear not: [there is nothing to fear] for I am with you; do not look around you in terror *and* be dismayed, for I am your God. I will strengthen *and* harden you [to difficulties]: yes, I will help you; yes, I will hold you up *and* retain you with My *victorious* right hand of rightness *and* justice.

(Isaiah 41:10 AMP)

When you pass through the waters I will be with you, and through the rivers they shall not overwhelm you; when you walk through the fire you shall not be burned *or* scorched, nor shall the flame kindle upon you.

(Isaiah 43:2 AMP)

Hear the words of Paul in Romans 8:38-39:

For I am persuaded beyond doubt—am sure—that neither death, nor life, nor angels, nor principalities, nor things impending *and* threatening, nor things to come, nor powers, nor height, nor depth, nor anything else in creation will be able to separate us from the love of God which is in Christ Jesus our Lord.

(Romans 8:38-39 AMP)

What do these verses say to us about our lives, our fears? During your most intense bout with fear allow your mind to become an echo chamber resounding with the words of Jesus: "Fear not. . . . fear not. . . . fear not."

2
Becoming All That God Wants You To Become

If you believe that you cannot get along in life without depending upon someone else, fear is guiding and directing your life. Some men believe they cannot get along without a woman to lean on or meet their needs. There are many women who feel the same way about men. The agoraphobic is *afraid* of people. Just the opposite is the person who feels he cannot live *without* people. The belief that you cannot live without another person is a sign of dependency. Being a dependent person strains your relationships with other people, indicates an inner fear, and also reflects the tone of your relationship with God.

Dependent people believe they can do things only with the assistance of others. A woman said, "I'd like to become more involved in church," but because she had no one to go with her she didn't. Her specific reasons were, "I'd hate to walk into a place alone," "I'm not the best conversationalist, and if I'm with someone, that person can carry the conversation," "What if someone is friendly and wants to get acquainted? I don't know what I would do," and "Most people go as a couple or family or with a friend. I'd feel out of place." This type of reasoning can lead to isolation in many situations. In the chart below, notice the difference between being dependent and being self-reliant.

	Dependency	Isolation	Self-Reliance
Interpersonal behavior	Leans on others. Other-directed	Avoids others. Social isolation.	Moves toward others. True relationship based on sense of independence.
Seen by others	Helpless. "Needy." Clinging.	Aloof. Narcissistic. Closed	Mature. Capable. Open.
Self-disclosure	Overdisclosure.	Underdisclosure.	Disclosures appropriate to situation.
Choices	Constricted range of choices.	Constricted range of choices.	Wide range of choices.
Feelings	Moves from one extreme to another. Feels helpless.	Typically flat. Feels alienated.	Appropriate to situation.
Fears	Fears being alone, becoming social isolate.	Fears being with others, becoming dependent.	Few interpersonal fears.

	Dependency	Isolation	Self-Reliance
Self-evaluation	Indirect self-acceptance based on others' opinions.	Indirect self-acceptance based on own achievements.	Direct self-acceptance. Minimal self-evaluation.
Assumptions	I need others. I can't work alone.	I don't need anybody. Others let me down.	I don't need others but I enjoy them.

How much do you want other people to do for you? Do you have to have others help you or be with you most of the time? You probably spend time rehearsing in your mind vivid memories of times you didn't enjoy yourself because you were not with someone. This kind of imaginative thinking will only serve to reinforce your fear (and begin to increase depression).

What can you do to become more of a self-reliant independent person? The first step is to honestly answer the question, "Do I want to become an independent self-reliant person?" A strange question? No, not at all. Many people say, "Yes, I want to change and live a more fulfilling life," but in reality they do not. Why? The cost of changing is too high, they feel, or they do not want to give up the benefits they are gaining from being dependent. They feel they are successful being dependent and they derive some benefit from this life-style. They are not sure they could be successful in a new life-style. Because the risk is too great they continue to live in fear and hesitancy.

What are the benefits of a life pattern of

dependency? A person may like to be taken care of. He may like to have decisions made for him and enjoy the security of confinement. But at the same time he hates himself for being that way. The effort and time involved in creating a new life-style may require too much effort. The person knows he will feel uncomfortable with a new life-style for awhile and feels sure he would create some of the same uneasy feelings in those around him.

And what if we try to change and are unsuccessful? For some the possibility of failure is worse than the discomfort they are experiencing in their dependency. Many people choose to live their lives in some form of paralysis. Paralyzed by fear and hesitancy, they remain emotionally crippled.

Jesus Christ asks you the same question he asked the man at the pool of Bethesda in John 5. "Do you want to be healed?" "Do you really want to change?" Here was a man who had been crippled and paralyzed for thirty-eight years. He was waiting for someone to put him into the water for healing but no one ever seemed to be available. Occasionally the water in this pool bubbled up or was troubled as the Scripture states. Jewish tradition said that when the water bubbled up an angel was troubling or stirring the water and those who were placed in the water were healed.

Does it seem a bit strange that a man who had waited at the pool for so many years could not find anyone to place him in the water at the appropriate time? Why did Jesus ask such an insightful and penetrating question instead of just touching the man and bringing about an instant healing? Listen to the dialogue between Jesus and this man in John 5:1-14 (AMP), and note some of the unique statements.

Later on there was a Jewish festival (feast), for which Jesus went up to Jerusalem.

2 Now there is in Jerusalem a pool near the Sheep Gate. This pool in the Hebrew is called Bethesda, having five porches (alcoves, collonnades, doorways).

3 In these lay a great number of sick folk, some blind, some crippled and some paralyzed (shriveled up), *waiting for the bubbling up of the water.*

5 There was a certain man there who had suffered with a deep-seated *and* lingering disorder for thirty-eight years.

6 When Jesus noticed him lying there helpless, knowing that he had already been a long time in that condition, He said to him, *Do you want to become well? [Are you really in earnest about getting well?]*

7 The invalid answered, Sir, I have nobody when the water is moving to put me into the pool; but while I am trying to come myself, somebody else steps down ahead of me.

8 Jesus said to him, *Get up; pick up* your bed (sleeping pad) *and walk!*

9 *Instantly* the man *became well and recovered his strength* and *picked up* his bed *and walked.* But that happened on the Sabbath.

10 So the Jews kept saying to the man that had been healed, It is the Sabbath and you have no right to pick up your bed — it is not lawful.

11 He answered them, The Man Who healed me *and* gave me back my strength, He Himself said to me, Pick up your bed and walk!

12 They asked him, Who is the Man Who told you, Pick up your bed and walk?

13 Now the invalid who had been healed did not know Who it was, for Jesus had quietly gone away (had passed on unnoticed), since there was a crowd in the place.

14 Afterward when Jesus found him in the temple, He said to him, See, you are well! Stop sinning, or something worse may happen to you.

What about the statement "Do you really want to become well?" (Are you really in earnest about getting well?) Are you in earnest about changing your life at this time regardless of what has occurred in the past?

This man gave Jesus a reason or excuse why he hadn't been healed. All of us have reasons why our lives are the same today as yesterday. We may believe our own reasons and see value, substance and logic in them. In fact we may have told ourselves these reasons for so long that we have come to regard them as fact.

Are you open to evaluating and challenging your reasons and beliefs? Are you willing to just consider another alternative and give it a possible look? What would it hurt? What would it cost? Perhaps nothing more than a bit of discomfort as we begin to shake off our false security system. It is better to purposefully shake it yourself than to have it crumble in an emotional earthquake sometime in the future.

Jesus Christ wants you to shake your own life, not be thrown about by others and circumstances. He wants you to control circumstances of your life in the midst of them, not to let circumstances control you.

Perhaps that is why Jesus did not listen to or accept the paralytic's reason for his condition. He appeared to have a very plausible excuse. And I'm sure he received acceptance and understanding from other people because of it. He probably gained pity, attention, and freedom from some of life's regular responsibilities because of his condition. Jesus did not respond at all to the man's reasons. He didn't even acknowledge it. Instead He gave him a directive! "Get up; pick up your bed and walk!" He is saying the same to each of us. He wants us to get up and walk through life without fear or hesitancy. And because He walks with us, we can.

Later Jesus ran into this man in the temple and He reinforced to him the fact that he was healed. "See, you are well." Jesus is saying the same thing to each of us: "You are well! Experience your wellness, your wholeness. Live! Use the resources you have. Live your life as though you were well."

And then Jesus said to the man, "Stop sinning, or something worse may happen to you!" Could sin be the cause for your fear and intimidation? "Not at all," you say. "I cannot help being the way I am. If you had experienced what I have gone through in my life, you would be fearful too! You didn't have my childhood. You didn't have my parents. Were you abused as I was? Have you been rejected as I have been? If you had, you wouldn't even suggest such a thought!''

At the heart of the misery and hurt of mankind, we find sin. Either our sin or the sin of another. We are not responsible for the actions of those who in the past have mistreated us. The emotional and traumatic hurt experienced at the hands of another is painful. So many children today bear the emotional scars of words and actions perpetrated upon them when they were helpless and vulnerable. The effects are carried with them for years.

But eventually we come to the time in life when we must decide whether to remain with the ghosts of the past roaming throughout our personality, or to do some housecleaning. ''I will always be this way,'' you say. ''There is no possibility of change. No hope.'' How do you know unless you are open to trying? Jesus said, ''Take the risk *before you* choose to live your life the way it is at the present time.'' You see, the responsibility for who and what we are does shift to us at some point in life. And we do have to face the question, ''Is my choice to remain fearful, intimidated, and hesitant what God is asking of me?'' Is it not a life of faith, dependent upon Him, which frees you up to be free of others? Are you choosing a limited existance?

His timetable for change may *not* be the same as the healing of the man at the pool. He knows that it will not be instant, *and* may be a gradual progression. But he says to us, ''Depend upon me, for your strength, discover our strength, your qualities, your potentials as I see them.''

Practice what Paul said in Philippians 4:13 (AMP), ''I have strength for all things in Christ Who empowers me—I am ready for anything and equal to anything through Him Who infuses inner strength into me, [that is, I am self-sufficient in Christ's sufficiency].

What are the benefits of becoming more self-sufficient? There are many. For one thing, your life of fear will disappear. You will be much more in charge of your feelings. You will experience normal responses and emotions but will have less tendency to overreact. Your self-image will begin to improve as you begin to see yourself standing on your own two feet. As you become more independent, as you do more on your own and for yourself, your feelings about yourself will change for the better.

You'll also become more efficient and productive. At first you may experience an inward struggle since you may have relied so much upon others. Before, you may (unknowingly) have been using your energy to get others to do things for you. This same time and energy can be used more productively now. One man used to spend over an hour a day at work getting others to do his tasks in areas he felt insecure about. No wonder his co-workers resented him and he failed to move ahead in his position.

An added benefit of being more independent is the ability to handle stress more effectively. You cannot change all the pressure and events around you, but emotional control and your new found feelings of self-confidence give you a better basis for handling the stress of life. Dependent people tend to become depressed, fearful and intimidated, or angry when they are under stress. Their inner control fades. But a self-sufficient person (through the power of Christ) experiences stability.

How does a person begin to break out of a pattern of dependency? First of all, describe in writing what you would like to change in your life at this time. Then write down the excuses or reasons you have given yourself to keep yourself from moving to a new direction. You have probably created a multitude of beliefs about yourself and life in general. Do you find yourself saying, "I can't do it by myself. . . . I have to be able to do it perfectly before I'll try it. . . . What if I get upset and fail? . . . What if others don't like me when I change?" It is important to establish your personal goals and then begin to eliminate the roadblocks which may hinder you. Any negative statements which you make to yourself must be challenged, countered, and changed.

Look at your assets and strengths. Focus on the areas where you *know* you have some abilities even though you feel you have weaknesses in other areas of your life. Making a list of these may seem tedious and boring but it is necessary. Then see yourself in your mind achieving these goals.

Norman Vincent Peale describes this process.
If setting worthy goals is the first step on the road to success, the second is the belief—no, the conviction—that you are capable of achieving those goals. There has to be in your mind the unshakable image of yourself succeeding at the goal you have set yourself. The

more vivid this image is, the more obtainable the goal becomes. Great athletes have always known this. The high jumper "sees" himself skimming over the bar; the golfer facing a difficult shot images the ball soaring over the intervening obstacles and landing squarely on the green; the placekicker in football keeps his head down as he kicks, but in his mind's eye he holds the mental picture of what he wants to happen in the next few seconds. He "sees" the great arena full of tense spectators, the onrushing defensive linemen, the blockers holding them off, the ball spiraling back to the holder, the thud as his foot connects with it at precisely the right angle, then its spinning flight squarely between the uprights. The more intensely he images this before it happens, the higher his confidence in himself and the better his chances of making it happen.[2]

Dr. Gary Emery has suggested asking a series of questions to discover your strengths and self-reliance.

1. Do I take care of my basic needs: cooking, clothing, transportation, housing?
2. Do I have my own source or potential source of money?
3. Are my emotions dependent on the actions of others or events outside myself?
4. Can I go out to social events, parties, meetings by myself?
5. Do I enjoy being alone with myself?
6. Can I make decisions on my own?
7. Do I trust my own judgment?
8. Do I have confidence in my taste?
9. Do I have close friends?

10   Can I accept help from others?

11.   Do I isolate myself from others?[3]

The answers to these questions may give you an indication of areas to work on. And did you realize that even the *action* of making a list is a positive step forward?

If this list did not indicate any areas of particular concern for you, identify some which *are* a problem. Based upon your responses, choose at least one situation a day in which you are going to change what you do in a dependent manner to an independent response. Each day increase the number of times you act in an independent way. What you choose to do should be a bit of a challenge but not overwhelming. Just focus on each behavior on that day and don't be concerned about the rest of the week.

Would you believe there is more? To stop now would be defeating the entire purpose so we need to go back to making a written record. Write down each time you behave in a more positive, independent manner. Describe how and what you did and how you felt about doing it. Was there much fear involved? Even if there was, you were still able to do it. Each time you do it you may notice it is easier.

Continue increasing the number of times each day you perform these new behaviors and note your feelings. As you continue to be consistent your motivation will increase. It will take time to overcome past fears and develop new strengths. But be patient and remember that God is working within you.

NOTES FOR CHAPTER TWO

[1]Dr. Gary Emery: A New Beginning: *How You Can Change Your Thoughts Through Cognitive Therapy*, (Simon and Schuster, N.Y.), 1981. Pg. 243.

[2]Norman Vincent Peale, *Dynamic Imaging*, (Fleming H. Revell, Old Tappan, N.J.), 1982. Pg. 85.

[3]Dr. Gary Emery, Adapted—Chapter 13.

3
Childhood Fears

Do you remember what it was like to be a child? Do you remember the fun and frivolity of childhood? All of us have memories, though some of them tend to fade with time. Some of the memories that may still be with us may be the fears we have held onto from our early years.

What did you fear as a child? Or, if you are a parent, what do your own children fear? And how do you respond to their fears? It would be safe to say that all children are afraid from time to time. Unfortunately some are fearful constantly. What we need to remember as adults is that most of the fears children have are learned! Children learn to fear bees, snakes, dogs, cats, heights, loud noises, and monsters. But how do they learn? What happens that makes them fearful?

The capacity to experience fear is part of our creation. Survival depends upon a blend of caution and boldness with neither being radical. Although most fears are learned, a few are basically innate. That which is unexpected creates fear. Infants are startled when they hear a sudden, intense noise. Similarly an infant knows its own family members, but it fears strangers. Fear of the unknown is common to both children and adults. It is the basis for many other fears. Because the person, thing, or object is unknown, we do not have control over it. Our fear is that it might control us. If we are in control we feel secure. Conversely, being out of control breeds insecurity. We either cower and retreat from the unknown or else attempt to destroy it.

We use fear as a protective response. Whenever you feel threatened you begin to feel fearful, and so does a child, especially as he begins to see himself as a person. A child soon learns what is safe and what is not. He learns this through firsthand experience and by observing the behavior of others. This fear response is a protection which children need. Often fear turns into anger and we attempt to defend ourselves. Through anger we lash back at whatever it is that is a threat to our existence.

Children learn their fears not only from their parents, but also from their friends and other adults such as teachers. A fearful adult tends to infect a child with his own particular fears.

Our actions have a greater effect on our children than the verbal instructions we give them. Children will watch how we respond to a threatening situation. If parents are overly protective of their child due to their own anxieties, the child may tend to be timid and fearful. Children who are encouraged to be risk takers and to experience what the world has to offer are less fearful. But if children are consistently cautioned about the dangers of life they tend to develop a large number of fears.

Many fears occur because of conditioning. They are learned through association. A child eats a piece of fruit and becomes deathly ill. He may have a fear of eating that fruit again. Another child has an accident while visiting the zoo and every time the suggestion is made to visit the zoo he begins to feel fearful.

Years ago one of the girls in my high school group shared her experience with cats. As a young child she was riding her tricycle around the block. Suddenly a cat emerged from one of the homes, came up to her and scratched her leg. After that every time she saw a cat or when someone suggested getting her one she became terrified. When I met her the fear was so intense that if someone brought a cat into the room she would literally bolt out the door.

As a child I had my tonsils taken out when I was six years of age. I was told that I would be in the hospital for two or three days and I would get to eat a lot of sherbet. Unfortunately, my adenoids bled for a week and I had a very unpleasant experience. For years whenever I would visit the doctor's office and smell some of the same smells as when I stayed in the hospital, I experienced a mild sense of anxiety. Many of our fears which we as adults have today were learned through association and then generalized to other situations or objects in our lives.

How do children learn to be afraid? It could be that they learn some of their fears from us! Impossible? No. Children learn through modeling or imitative learning. They like to imitate adults who are important to them. I may tell my child not to be afraid of going to the doctor, but if he sees me sitting in the waiting room anxious, palms sweaty, thinking of ways to cancel the appointment, he will know that I am afraid.

Unfortunately, one other way in which children learn to fear is by being rewarded for their fear. Perhaps a parent allows a child to get out of certain responsibilities or obligations because of his fear. Or maybe the child learns that he can receive a great deal of attention from his parents and friends by appearing fearful. Some children greatly exaggerate their fear because of all the attention they receive. I have seen children walk into a yard with a small dog and be perfectly at ease around the animal when no adults are present. The same children with the same dog may behave much differently when adults are there to see their "so-called" fear. Children have been known to either stop or start crying depending upon whether or not a parent is watching. We as parents can condition our child's fears by paying too much attention to their behavior.

What do children fear? Are there common anxieties which most children experience? Yes, there are. Perhaps by being aware of them we can learn to relax a bit and not inadvertently reinforce their fears. Children's fears come and go but they do seem to follow a pattern. Let's look at the fears of different ages of children.

One of the most common fears of the *pre-school* child is separation. This is usually directed toward separation from mother or both parents. In some cases even moving brings these separation fears. They also fear monsters, ghosts, creatures which they imagine, many types of animals, dreams, darkness, and going to bed.

Children from the age of *six to eight* are concerned about their bodies being hurt or even about their bodies changing. Being sick, experiencing pain or hurt, bad dreams, thunder, and death are quite common fears. Fear of animals is still common but now the fears become specific, perhaps toward a particular animal, whereas preschool children tend to fear animals in general. The older child, *eight to twelve* has similar fears of being injured or becoming ill. But some new fears arise also related to how he is doing in school and his physical appearance.

And then *adolescence* hits. Now the fears are centered more around interpersonal relationships instead of intrapersonal. The adolescent compares himself with others in terms of physical features, performance, mental ability, etc. Body shape, pimples, strange feelings in his body and thoughts in his head replace fears of animals, the dark and dreams. Self-concept is the core around which many of his fears evolve. As a child grows and develops, the fears move from being general to specific and from fantasy to reality.

How do you recognize your child's fears? What are the indications that anxiety is present? Some children are very verbal about their fears and you have little difficulty being aware. Others either avoid thinking about them or make it a point not to share their fears. But if a child is quite fearful or troubled with anxiety you might begin to notice some of the following symptoms emerging.

Children who have difficulty concentrating and either become listless or hyper may be struggling with some inner anxiety. If their appetite changes from eating very little to consuming greater amounts of food, this too could be a sign of anxiety. Behaviors such as bed wetting, nightmares, restlessness, insomnia, being overly talkative, not talking, stuttering, experiencing panic attacks, developing compulsive behaviors or obsessive thought patterns are additional indications of fear. Often a wide range of bodily complaints will be the indication of fear or may accompany many of the above.

Let's look in greater detail at some of these childhood fears and what can be done about them. For many children an animal is a fear object. (It is for many adults as well.) How do you help a child who is afraid of an animal? You don't force the child to face the fear all at once, for he does not have the resources to cope with it. Let's assume that a child is afraid of cats. Even though cats look harmless their claws are sharp. A cat may appear small to us but look at it from the child's point of view. A thiry-pound child looking at a fifteen-pound cat sees something different than you do. Imagine a cat half of or a third of your weight and your response might be a bit more cautious. A cat also bites and is unpredictable. How do you then help a child? (The following approach can be used with many other animals as well.)

Don't have the child face his fear all at once. Instead try gradual exposure. Show the child pictures of a cat or point out the qualities of cats on the various ads on television. Let a child watch you enjoy handling a cat or the picture of a cat. Let the child know that he can pet the cat as you do. Don't force him to do so, but when he does touch the cat talk about how soft the cat's fur is, how pretty it is, etc. It is important to select a cat that is calm, and responds positively to love and attention. Encourage the child to pet the cat with you more and more frequently. The time will come when the child is able to do this on his own and be spontaneous about it.

Some parents have found it helpful to have the child keep a written record of his progress regarding whatever it is that he fears. Such a written record shows the child he is attaining a goal. The record might indicate when the child responded to a cat, how long, where, and his positive feelings.

Nighttime fears such as fear of the dark and nightmares are very common. When you or I take a fear to bed with us it often crops up again in our dreams. Our minds run wild during our sleep. Darkness can be frightening, for it generates fears of being isolated, left alone, abandoned, or being lost. A gradual approach once again can be helpful with a child. A child needs to know that it is all right to talk about his fears, that he will not be made fun of for being fearful. You might try gradually reducing the amount of light in the child's room. Share with the child and commit to memory the following verse: "When you lie down you shall not be afraid; yes, you shall lie down and your sleep shall be sweet. Be not afraid of sudden terror *and* panic, nor of the stormy blast *or* the storm and ruin of the wicked when it comes [for you will be guiltless]. For the Lord shall be your confidence, firm *and* strong and shall keep your foot from being caught [in a trap or hidden danger]" (Proverbs 3:24-26 AMP).

Many children have nightmares or, as they call them, "bad dreams" three to six times a month. Persistent and repetitive nightmares may indicate excessive tension, stress or fear during the day. Dreams which occur nightly or several times a night may be telling you something. (For specific and detailed help with children's fears see *Helping the Fearful Child* by Dr. Jonathan Kellerman, W.W. Norton and Company.)

Earlier we mentioned that children *learn* most of their fears. This means that it is also possible to *unlearn* them. Dr. Kellerman suggests a number of practical and workable ways to help children rid their lives of fear.

1. Let the child know that it is all right to be afraid. Everyone has fears at some time in his life. A certain amount of fear is normal and we don't have to be ashamed when we are afraid. Share your own childhood fears and let the child know, too, that those fears passed from your life. This can be an encouragement to him.

2. Help the child understand that being afraid is temporary. He may even fear that his fear will last forever. Children need to have a message of hope for the future.

3. Let the child know that it is right and good to talk about his fear. Sharing his fear helps him keep the fear in perspective and avoid distortions. It helps you know the extent of the fear so you can help him overcome any distortions. Many parents have found it helpful to have the child draw his feelings or fears on a piece of paper with crayons, or act out his fantasies, or use puppets to talk out his fears.

4. Let the child know that it is also normal *not* to be afraid. When a child can observe another person not being afraid in a situation where he is fearful, he gets the message that it is possible not to be afraid.

5. Help the child learn a new response or behavior to replace his fear response. These are called *counter behaviors* or *fear replacing behaviors*. Encourage the child to imagine himself not being afraid in his usual fear experience. Positive imageries are powerful substitutes which we could all use to greater effectiveness. Even encouraging a child to become angry in his fear situation can be

beneficial. It is difficult to be fearful and angry at the same time. The anger will give him a greater feeling of control. Participating in a positive activity or favorite pastime when the feared object or situation is at hand can eventually lessen the fear.

As with adults, so it is with children — repeated facing of a fear is the best method of overcoming it. We all need to use the creative powers of our God-given imagination so we can visualize ourselves handling the fearful event. Depending upon the comprehension level of the child, selected portions of Scriptures (found elsewhere in this book) will help bring peace and comfort to his mind.

But what about your fears? Are they fears which are still remaining from your childhood? Are they fears which you have carried and cultivated for many years? If so, what are some steps you can take to unlearn these fears? There will be some specific suggestions for you to consider in the later chapters.

One of the underlying themes of fear for both children and adults is the fear of the unknown. We desire certainty. We want to be assurred that we will be all right, that we will be safe, that our questions are answered, that we will be able to do what we are asked to do.

Many of our other specific fears have their roots in this fear. We may not know all that will happen, but God does know. The Psalmist says, "Thou knowest my downsitting and mine uprising, thou understandest my thought afar off." (Psalm 139:2). One of the great lessons of life is to come to the place where we can say,

"It is all right for me not to have all of the answers or to know what is going to happen. I will do what I can and learn to rest in the promises of what God has said." Forcing oneself to actually do this while visualizing the presence of Jesus Christ standing next to us in the unknown situation facing us does give a security and peace.

4

Fear and Phobias

A phobia is a special kind of fear which is out of proportion to the situation. It is beyond voluntary control, and cannot be reasoned or explained away. What happens is that a person avoids whatever it is he fears. He cannot stop his phobia and he knows his fear is unrealistic. You have probably met people who are phobic. At times it is difficult to comprehend why they respond in the way they do or why they are so fearful! Their fear seems totally inappropriate.

An example of a phobia is the woman who was terrified of bees. She went to great pains to make sure the windows were closed and sealed in her home and even wore a net over her head whenever she went into the backyard. She injured herself several times by overreacting when she saw a bee nearby. Once she turned quickly to avoid a bee and ran into a tree. Another time she sprained her ankle. One particularly embarrassing moment occurred when she was seated at a table for an outdoor luncheon near a pool. A bee flew near the table and then lighted on the center bouquet. The woman took one look and jumped up, pushing her chair over. As she turned to walk away she moved too quickly and bumped into another table, spilling most of the beverages. Embarrassed, she made another turn and plunged into the pool! Each time she had an experience like this it increased her fear even more. She would agonize in her mind anticipating her next encounter with a bee.

Similarly, an older man who had been somewhat fearful of water most of his life became increasingly afraid of water. He used to sometimes wade in water and had been in a boat and canoe on several occasions. One day he slipped in a pool and swallowed a great quantity of water. He panicked and it took him several hours to calm down. From that point on he refused to get on any boat whether large or small. He would not even sit close to a pool or any other body of water. No amount of reasoning or explanation by others had any effect upon him.

Both individuals in these examples follow the typical pattern of people with phobias. They are people on edge, constantly on the lookout for their own particular fear. Because of this over-concern they live a life of restriction. Pre-planned avoidance is part of their daily routine. They are constantly watching for whatever is being associated with their phobia. Their vision is greatly refined. A bug phobic checks around the cupboards and corners of any strange room for fear of discovering a bug. But there are so many things which cannot be avoided. Crossing streets, bridges, elevators, thunderstorms, dogs, cats, birds, crowds—how can these be completely avoided unless you limit your life and become a recluse! That is usually what happens.

Do you identify with this problem or find it hard to understand? It does appear strange that some could be afraid of some of the most common everyday things of life. If you have never experienced a phobia, it will be difficult for you to understand how intense and terrifying the experience is for a phobic.

Terror is a very apt description. Our tendency is to say to the phobic, "That's ridiculous. It's silly to be afraid of that. Grow up." But this does nothing to help the phobic overcome his dread. Because of our lack of understanding and constructive help, phobics are often sensitive and ashamed of their fears. The fear of ridicule puts a damper on sharing their fears with others. They begin to feel they're the only ones who feel this way and an additional fear may develop that they are going crazy! By keeping the problem a secret the phobic limits his chances of discovering what to do about it. The energy which could be used to solve the problem is used by running from it. Thus the fear is perpetuated.

One of the most common and distressing of all phobias for adults is *agoraphobia*. The literal meaning of the word is "fear of the marketplace." It was first used a hundred years ago by the German psychiatrist, Westphal, to describe the "impossibility of walking through certain streets or square or possibility of so doing only with resultant dread or anxiety."

Today this term is used to describe fears of going into public places such as cars, buses, shops, crowds, theaters, churches, etc. This malady is rare in children and usually begins in adults between the ages of eighteen and thirty-five. It often developes after a major upset in a person's life. This could include such things as an unpleasant scene in a public place, serious illness of oneself or another, danger, leaving home, death of a loved one, engagement, marriage, or whatever. Sometimes something quite trivial triggers this fear.

Many agoraphobics conceal their problem over a period of time. The condition can occur suddenly within a few hours or it may take years to develop. It usually begins with reoccurring attacks of anxiety while away from home. Intensity of the panic can be such that the person is glued to the same spot until the panic subsides. At this time the individual usually wants to go home to safety. Often there is a definite aversion of returning to the spot where this occurred. Anxiety and depression are the emotional response. The problem may occur again soon or months may go by before another episode.

When these upsets continue to occur, the person, usually a woman, may seek medical assistance, but all that can be found are some signs of anxiety. In time she may begin to avoid certain events or locales for fear she might have another bad experience. A possible sequence may proceed in this way: A woman travels to work each day on an express bus with very few stops. Because she cannot get off immediately when panic occurs, she begins to take the regular street bus. When panic occurs here she begins to walk, then limits her walking to close to home, then to her yard, then to the house itself. Does this sound extreme? Perhaps. But many people struggle silently with this for years.

This condition can also affect interpersonal relationships if the agoraphobic feels better only in the presence of someone (or an animal or object) she trusts. Their presence gives her a greater peace of mind. But she may become almost possessive since she needs constant companionship. Serious strain in a relationship may occur. She may develop ways to lessen her fear, such as carrying certain objects wherever she goes, chewing gum, selecting deserted streets or buses to walk or ride.

Most of the afflicted live with their families so the condition affects more than one person. Their restrictions they place on themselves place a strain on the others. Often the agoraphobic requires an escort wherever she goes, or other family members must do all the shopping and errands. One agoraphobic woman who had been married for over sixteen years had arranged her life so carefully that during this entire time she had never been alone more than a few minutes.

Can the agoraphobic be cured? Does motivation or willpower help? To a certain degree it helps, but it is not enough. The major task is to reduce anxiety to a level low enough for the person's willpower to complete his own treatment. What will help reduce the anxiety level? Exposure to the situation until the person becomes accustomed to it. The exposure process can take several hours and must be repeated several times.

An example of how this process occurs is seen in the case of Janice, a married women who had not been able to leave her house for fifteen years without her husband. She desperately wanted to be free from this difficulty and specifically wanted to be able to cross a busy street by herself and shop in some stores close to her home.

The counselor began treatment by taking Janice to the road near her home and helping her cross. This was repeated several times and then the counselor gradually left her side, staying first a few yards away and then further away until she did the crossing on her own. After an hour-and-a-half she felt fairly comfortable and much calmer about crossing the road. She committed herself to practice crossing roads of similar traffic density near her home. On her next session with the counselor she made several trips alone while he watched from a distance. She still felt panic and often held on to other people as she crossed the street. She began to ride to work on the bus instead of riding in a car with a friend. Between sessions she took longer and longer walks and bus rides. After eight sessions with the counselor she was able to go out regularly without any anxiety and her improvement was quite substantial. Here again we find the same principle in operation: To overcome a fear, it must be faced!

There is one further suggestion I would add to this approach. That is the use of positive imagination. So often an agoraphobic will visualize the dreaded scene in her mind in a negative manner. She reinforces her fear by playing the scene over and over, working herself into a greater panic. This process can be reversed, however, by visualizing the scene in a *positive* manner. The individual should sit in a comfortable chair, become fully relaxed, then begin to visualize herself strolling across the street and into the shops. But in her mind she needs to see two people walking and strolling—herself and the Person of Jesus Christ. By imagining and sensing His presence during this time, by playing the scene over and over in a positive imaging, her confidence can be strengthened. She may have to approach this gradually as she does the actual encounter with the street and crowds, but the encounter in her mind can be expanded each time as well.

We are not born with phobias. We develop, cultivate, and allow them to control our lives. But they are not permanent guests, only visitors for as long as we allow them to dwell with us. Eviction may take effort, but it is possible!

5
Worry—What is it?

Why does the Word of God say so much about worry? Does God expect us to have a problem with worry? Yes, He does. You and I have a built in tendency to imagine the worst instead of the best. It is a carry-over from the fall of man.

Worry is the state of being at war with oneself, and every one of us has the capacity of carrying on his own individual war. In describing this conflict the author of Proverbs says that "Anxiety in a man's heart weighs it down" (Proverbs 12:25 AMP). Worry impairs our attention. In worry we pre-image the future. It is our futile attempt to control the future, but it results in failure. The failure brings with it a number of physical symptoms such as headaches, backaches, perspiration, weakness and fatigue, shortness of breath, constriction in the chest, indigestion, diarrhea, menstrual irregularity, insomnia, and muscular tension.

Is all worry and anxiety bad? What is the creative aspect to worry and anxiety? One minister has said, ". . . not all anxiety is destructive. There is a creative form of anxiety which causes a man to get out of bed in the morning and go to work. A mother answers the cry of her child in response to an inner anxiety which is also creative. (Sudden danger) stimulates the secretion of additional adrenalin into the bloodstream and prepares us for "fight or flight." This is a God-given instinctual response to fear. It is only when fear becomes an all-pervasive anxiety which impairs our effectiveness that it ceases to be creative and becomes destructive."[1]

Dr. Quentin Hyder, a Christian psychiatrist, also suggests that:

All anxiety or psychic tension is not bad, however. A little of it in normal amounts can enhance performance. Athletes would be unable to perform successfully without it. Businessmen do better in their competitive world than they could do without its stimulus. It definitely strengthens concentration and spurs imagination, thereby producing more creative ideas. It stimulates interest and develops ambition. It protects from danger. Too much, however, can actually decrease performance.[2]

These men have been talking about anxiety in its healthy form. Worry, however, is different. It has no such creative element. But isn't there such a thing as concern? Is it the same as worry? No, it is not.

Concern is often good and desirable. Concern

is usually focused on a specific problem (will my son be drafted, will my daughter marry the right man, or will there be a general economic depression). Although a sense of fear is present in "concern" there is primarily uneasiness, unhappiness, and greater personal identification with the problem than with pure fear states. Such concern often leads to attempts at a solution of the problem; if my son goes to college, he may be deferred from military service. If I give many parties, will my daughter have a better chance of meeting the right person? If I write to my congressman about overspending, will that help ward off a business depression? Worry, however is primarily apprehension (fear), agitation (fear), and anxiety (fear), with relatively little self-control. "Concern" binds man to man and furnishes the motive power that stimulates corrective action. Worry turns inward and often paralyzes action.[3]

Paster Earl Lee, whose son was one of the hostages in Iran, wrote:

Tension is normal and natural in life. Without tension we could not exist any more than a violin string can be played without being stretched across the bridge. This creative tension is not the same thing as destructive worry. Worry is like racing an automobile engine while it is in neutral. The gas and noise and smog do not get us anywhere. But legitimate concern (creative tension) is putting the car into low gear on your way to moving ahead. You tell yourself that you are going to use the power God has given you to do something about the situation which could cause you to fret.[4]

Worry immobilizes a person whereas concern moves one to overcome the problem.

What are the causes of anxiety? What do most people worry about? Four possible causes are the following: 1. Repressed anger creates anxiety; 2. Having unrealistic standards set for us or setting them ourselves can create this tension; 3. Situations in which a person must make a choice create anxiety; 4. Unresolved or undealt-with guilt also creates tremendous tension.

What do people worry about? It would be safe to say everything. Dr. Samuel Kraines suggests three categories into which most worries fall.

1. Disturbing situations for which one must find a solution; for example, how to obtain money for food, lodging, or medical expenses.

2. Disturbing situations over which one has no control; for example, a mother dying of cancer; a usually prompt daughter who is five hours "late;" or a son in active combat.

3. Unimportant, insignificant, minor problems of everyday life which warrant little attention, let alone "worry." People "worry" about minor details of everyday life, concocting horrible possibilities, and then "stewing" about them. The housewife "worries" that she cannot clean the house as she once did, does not iron the clothes well, and cannot prepare proper

meals. The man "worries" that he is doing poorly at work, that he will be "fired" and that he "cannot pay his bills." The list goes on and on. The worry is not only a feeling tone of fearfulness but an overriding sense of futility, hopelessness, and dreaded possibilities.[5]

Earl Nightengale once shared a study on what people worry about, and found that forty percent of our worries are about things that never happen. How many things have you worried about that never happened?

The researcher found that thirty percent of people's worries concern things that are in the past, that can't be changed by worry. A person will think, "Oh, good grief, why did I ever do that? Why did I ever say that? If only I had come from the right sort of home, these things wouldn't have happened to me." He spends time going over and over some experience of the past and worrying about its lasting effects on his life.

Twelve percent of our worries about our health are needless. You get up in the morning, feeling not quite up to par, and you wonder if you're coming down with something. "I ran into that man with that strange cough yesterday—I wonder if I picked it up." Though we often need to have more positive concern about caring properly for our bodies, plain worry doesn't accomplish anything, and can be detrimental.

Ten percent of our worries the researcher designated as "petty, miscellaneous worries"—not worth worrying about. That leaves a total of eight percent for real, legitimate concerns.

How do people develop the habit pattern of worrying? It starts as a fleeting negative thought passing through your mind. It is repeated time and time again and soon it cuts a channel through your mind like a newly formed stream cuts through a sand bar. Each repetition and every detail deepens the tendency and broadens the channel. You ask the question "what if?" and you answer it. You ask it the second time but your answer now has more details. Each time your response grows more vivid.

There are many scriptural references and descriptions of the effects of fear and anxiety.

—"A tranquil mind gives life to the flesh" (Proverbs 14:30 RSV).

—"All the days of the desponding afflicted are made evil [by anxious thoughts and foreboding], but he who has a glad heart has a continual feast [regardless of circumstances]," (Proverbs 15:15 AMP).

—"A happy heart is a good medicine *and* a cheerful mind works healing, but a broken spirit dries the bones," (Proverbs 17:22 AMP).

—"A glad heart makes a cheerful countenance, but by sorrow of heart the spirit is broken," (Proverbs 15:13 AMP).

The final results of anxiety are negative, self-defeating, and incapacitating. What do we accomplish by worrying? Make a list of the things you worry about and then describe specifically what the worry has or will accomplish. Does it solve the problem—or does it create more problems? When a person worries about a problem, real or imaginary, it usually impedes him from being able to do something effective about it.

Worrying intensely about the possibility of some event happening not only does not prevent it from happening but can help to bring it about! A young seminary student is waiting to preach his first sermon. He sits thinking about what he is going to say. He begins to worry about forgetting words, about stumbling over certain phrases, and not presenting himself in a confident manner. As he continues to worry he actually visualizes himself making these mistakes. He actually sees himself failing, and the more he goes over and over this in his mind the more mistakes he sees himself making as he anticipates getting up to preach this sermon. And then when he does get up to preach he actually does make those mistakes that he worried about!

If you were to tell him that he shouldn't worry about his preaching he would reply, ''I was justified in worrying. After all, those problems that I worried about were real problems. They happened, didn't they? I should have been worried!'' What he does not realize is that by his own worry he actually helped them occur. He was responsible for his failure. He spent more time seeing himself failing than he did visualizing himself succeeding or overcoming the problem.

The principle here is that if you spend time seeing yourself as a failure or failing you will more than likely follow that example in your performance. You actually condition yourself for that kind of performance because of your negative thinking. However, if you spend that same amount of time and energy planning how to overcome those anticipated mistakes and visualize yourself being successful, your performance will be far better. Our thinking pattern affects how we perform. Proverbs says that "As a man thinketh in his heart so is he" (Proverbs 23:7).

Does worry have any place in the life of the Christian? Is worry or anxiety a sin? A slight amount of anxiety or tension, as mentioned earlier, is healthy. A person, however, who experiences extreme states of anxiety may not be able to control them. There may be many deep hidden feelings or hurts that have lingered for years and move about in the unconscious. A person may feel he is at the mercy of these feelings because he cannot pin down exactly why he is so anxious. However, if a person suffers from anxiety for very long, perhaps there may be a problem of sin because he has failed to face the problem, discover the roots of his feelings, and replace them with the healing power and resources offered through Jesus Christ and Scripture.

Anxiety may stem from unconscious feelings. Worry, however, is an ineffective method of coping with life. Oswald Chambers has said that all our fret and worry is caused by calculating without God. Worry actually implies the absence of trust. Since Scripture gives such direct answers to the problem of worry and actually tells us not to worry, this lack of trust in the Lord is certainly sin. Freedom from worry is possible. The answer lies in Scripture.

Therefore I tell you, stop being perpetually uneasy (anxious and worried) about your life, what you shall eat *or what you shall drink*, and about your body, what you shall put on. Is not life greater [in quality] than food, and the body [far above and more excellent] than clothing? Look at the birds of the air; they neither sow nor reap nor gather into barns, and yet your heavenly Father keeps feeding them. Are you not worth more than they? And which of you by worrying *and* being anxious can add one unit of measure [cubit] to his stature *or* to the span of his life? And why should you be anxious about clothes? Consider the lilies of the field *and* learn thoroughly how they grow; they neither toil nor spin; Yet I tell you, even Solomon in all his magnificence (excellence, dignity and grace) was not arrayed like one of these. But if God so clothes the grass of the field, which today is alive *and* green and tomorrow is tossed into the furnace, will He not much more surely clothe you, O you men with little faith? Therefore do not worry *and* be anxious, saying, What are we going to have to eat? or, What are we going to have to drink? or, What are we going to have to wear? For the Gentiles (heathen) wish for *and* crave *and* diligently seek after these things; and your heavenly Father well knows that you need them all. But seek for (aim at and strive after) first of all His kingdom, and His righteousness [His way of doing and being right], and then all these things taken together will be given you besides. So do not worry or be anxious about tomorrow, for tomorrow will have worries *and* anxieties of its own. Sufficient for each day is its own trouble; (Matthew 6:25-34 AMP).

From this passage we can discover several principles to help us overcome anxiety and worry. First, note that Jesus did not say, "If everything is going all right for you and there are no problems then stop worrying." He did not say, "If you feel like it then do not worry." He simply and directly said to stop worrying about your life. Perhaps in a way Jesus was saying that we should learn to accept situations that cannot be altered at the present time. This does not mean that we are to sit back and make no attempt to improve conditions around us, but we must face them and admit that this is the way they are. Learn how to live with them for the present.

Second, Jesus said that you cannot add any length of time to your life by worry. But you can take years off your life by worry and anxiety. The physical result of worry can actually shorten your life span.

A third suggestion made is that what we worry about may be part of the difficulty. It could be that our sense of values is distorted and that what we worry about should not be the center of our attention. The material items that seem so important should be secondary.

Christ also recommends that we practice living a day at a time. It is not possible to relive the past or to change what occurred in the past. Perhaps some of the results of the past can be changed, but some cannot. At any rate, worry certainly is not the solution. Nor is it possible to predict the future. We can prepare as best as possible for it, but even then we still must wait. The effect of worry will inhibit the potential of what can occur in the future.

Past experience does indicate several factors concerning worry. First of all, most of the events about which people worry do not happen. Look at the list of items you have worried over. Did they ever happen? Of course, now and then a person will say, "Yes, every one of these came true." Perhaps the reason for that is because of the worry. If you worried about failing, your energy was directed toward failing.

A second element of worry is that the anticipation of certain events that are inevitable usually is more distressing than the actual experience. Someone has said that anticipation is the magnifying glass of the emotions.

And third, even if an event is as serious as its anticipation it is possible to discover unsuspected resources to meet it. The Christian especially has resources for strength and stability at all times. Perhaps the manner in which we are able to be sustained in time of difficulty can be illustrated by looking at another passage of Scripture.

In Matthew 14:25-30 we find the disciples in a boat and Jesus walking toward them on the water. Peter saw Jesus and He invited Peter to come to Him. So Peter began to walk toward Jesus. He was fine until he saw the wind and then he became afraid and started to sink. If Peter had kept his eyes and mind upon Christ (the source of strength and the solution) he would have been all right. But Peter focused upon the wind and the rising waves stirred up by the wind (the problem or the negative aspect). He became overwhelmed by the problem even though he could have made it safely to Jesus! Worry is like that. We focus so hard on the problems that we take our eyes off the solution and thus create more difficulties for ourselves. We can be sustained in the midst of any difficulty by relying upon Jesus Christ.

The important principle to remember from these two passages of Scripture is this: We must learn to live a day at a time and accept certain situations and deal with them a step at a time. Worry should not be allowed because it does not solve the problem. And in the midst of our situation our main focus should be on Jesus Christ and not the difficulty.

In I Peter 5:7 another resource for worry is presented: "Casting all your care (or anxieties) upon Him; for He careth for you." This passage tells us what we are to do and then why we are to do it. Cast means to give up, or as one translations puts it, "Unload all your cares on Him." Cast actually means "having deposited with" and refers here to a direct and one-for-all committal to God of all that would give a person concern. The word "care" means anxiety or worry. All worries are to be cast upon the Lord so that when problems arise in the future that would have caused us to worry we will not worry about them.

The reason we can cast these cares on God with confidence is that God cares for us. We can be certain that, because He cares for us, He will strengthen us. He is not out to break us down but to help us stand firm. He knows our limits. "A bruised reed He will not break, and a dimly burning wick He will not quench" (Isaiah 42:3 RSV). The principle of this verse is: You can unload and give over every worry to God and because of His care and love He will strengthen you for any difficulty.

Another Old Testament passage clarifies what a person should do if he is to be free of worry in his life. As in Isaiah 26:3, He will keep you in perfect peace whose mind (or imagination) is stayed on Thee.

What we choose to think about will affect our actions and inner calmness. Those who suffer with worry choose to wrestle with negative thoughts or anticipate the worst. What goes on within our imagination creates the anxiety feelings. If your mind or imagination is centered about God—what He has done and will do for you—if it is centered upon the promises of Scripture, peace of mind is inevitable. But you must choose to center your thoughts in this way. God has made the provision but you must take the action. Freedom from every worry and anxiety is available but you must lay hold of it. The principle here is: Learn to direct your thoughts toward God and His teachings and you will never need to worry.[6]

What can I think about? What can I meditate upon? Here are passages which give us strength.

—"The eternal God is *thy* refuge, and underneath *are* the everlasting arms" (Deuteronomy 33:27).

—"But they that wait upon the Lord shall renew their strength; they shall mount up with wings as eagles; they shall run, and not be weary; and they shall walk, and not faint" (Isaiah 40:31).

—"The Lord is my shepherd; I shall not want" (Psalm 23:1).

—"I will fear no evil; for thou *art* with me; thy rod and thy staff comfort me" (Psalm 23:4).

—"If God *be* for us, who *can be* against us?" (Romans 8:31).

—"For I am persuaded, that neither death, nor life, nor angels, nor principalities, nor powers, nor things present, nor things to come, nor height, nor depth, nor any other creature, shall be able to separate us from the love of God, which is in Christ Jesus our Lord" (Romans 8:38,39).

—"But my God shall supply all your needs according to his riches in glory by Christ Jesus"(Philippians 4:19).

—I can do all things through Christ which strengtheneth me" (Philippians 4:13).

—"I have learned, in whatsoever state I am, *therewith* to be content" (Philippians 4:11).

—"Take therefore no thought for the morrow: for the morrow shall take thought for the things of itself. Sufficient unto the day *is* the evil thereof" (Matthew 6:34).

—"For God hath not given us the spirit of fear; but of power, and of love, and of a sound mind" (II Timothy 1:7).

—"We know that all things work together

for good to them that love God, to them who are the called according to *His* purpose" (Romans 8:28).

—"My grace is sufficient for thee: for my strength is made perfect in weakness" (II Corinthians 12:9).

—"When I am weak, then am I strong" (II Corinthians 12:10).

—"Like as a father pitieth his children, so the Lord pitieth them that fear him" (Psalm 103:13).

—"God *is* our refuge and strength, a very present help in trouble" (Psalm 46:1).

—"The Lord of hosts *is* with us; the God of Jacob is our refuge" (Psalm 46:11).

NOTES FOR CHAPTER FIVE

[1]Original source unknown.

[2]O. Quentin Hyder, *The Christians Handbook of Psychiatry*, (Fleming H. Revell Company, Old Tappan, N.J.).

[3]Kraines, Samuel H. and Thetford, Elois S., *Help for the Depressed*, (Courtesy of Charles C. Thomas, Publisher, Springfield, Illinois), 1972 pg. 191.

[4]Earl Lee, *Recycled for Living* (Regal Books, Ventura, Ca.) 1973 pg. 4.

[5]Kraines, pg. 190-191.

[6]H. Norman Wright, *The Christian Use of Emotional Power* (Fleming H. Revell, Old Tappan, N.J.), 1974. Pg. 61, 62.

6

Controlling Your Worry

A clear pattern for reducing and even eliminating anxiety is given in Philippians 4:6-9 (AMP):

Do not fret or have any anxiety about anything, but in every circumstance and in everything by prayer and petition [definite requests] with thanksgiving continue to make your wants known to God. And God's peace [be yours . . . that peace] which transcends all understanding, shall garrison and mount guard over your hearts and minds in Christ Jesus. For the rest, brethren, whatever is true, whatever is pure, whatever is lovely and honorable and seemly, whatever is just, whatever is pure, whatever lovely and lovable, whatever is kind and winsome and gracious, if there is any virtue and excellence, if there is anything worthy of praise, think on and weigh and take account of these things—fix your minds on them. Practice what you have learned and received and heard and seen in me, *and* model your way of living on it, and the God of peace—of untroubled, undisturbed well being—will be with you.

The people to whom Paul wrote these words had numerous problems. They had developed the pattern of worrying. Paul was very direct when he wrote to them. His words *Do not worry about anything* mean not even *one* thing. We are not asked to stop worrying if we feel like it or can see our way clear. It requires a definite act on our part to cease doing it. Verse nine is so important; it tells us to *practice* what we have learned. Many people make an effort to do as the Bible says, but they try it just once and then say, "It doesn't work." You've got to do it over and over again—you've got to *practice* living God's way.

One way to practice thinking God's way is to take a 3 x 5 card and on one side write the word "STOP" in big letters. On the other side of the card write out Philippians 4:6-9. Keep the card available in your pocket or in your purse. Whenever you begin to worry, pull out the card. If you are at home or in a place where no one else is around, hold the card in front of you and say the word "STOP" out loud. Then turn it over and read the Scripture out loud. If you are in the presence of others, read it to yourself so you don't give them the impression that you are strange!

The action of taking out that card and reading it will stop your worrying and will focus your mind on the positive input from the Scripture. This breaks the cycle of worry. The longer you let worry go on, the more difficult it is to stop;

you must do something tangible to break the pattern. ''But I have so many negative and worrisome thoughts which continually creep into my mind,'' you say, or ''I can't stop thinking!''

People think continually. We use our thoughts to check on our feelings and our behavior. Our thoughts tell us what to do and how to feel, they move us into action, and they also help us anticipate events. But often our thoughts use us. Right now you are thinking. You may be thinking, ''I don't understand this,'' or you may be thinking ''this does make some sense to me.''

Many of our thoughts are automatic. We do not have to think about thinking about them. They just seem to pop into our mind without any conscious effort. Are your automatic thoughts positive or are they negative? Most people who worry or are depressed have automatic thoughts which are negative. And the characteristic of negative thoughts is that they are generally wrong. They do not reflect reality. Instead, they reflect our insecurity, our feelings of inadequacy and our fears. You don't really want your automatic thoughts, they just appear out of nowhere. And usually they are exaggerated negative conclusions about your future, your daily world, and yourself. If you have negative thoughts and give into them, you will become more worrisome, more upset and more depressed. Look at the examples given below[1] of negative thoughts which either jump into our mind or which we consciously conjure up. As you read each one, indicate in the space provided whether you have these thoughts and then write an example of the most recent one.

**Thinking
Errors**

Type of Error	Examples	I have had this type of thought	Example
Personalizing	Thinking all situations and events revolve around you. "Everyone was looking at me and wondering why I was there."	_____	
Magnifying	Blowing negative events out of proportion. "This is the worst thing that could happen to me."	_____	
Minimizing	Glossing over the saving and positive factors. Overlooking the fact that "nothing really happened."	_____	
Either/Or Thinking	"Either I'm a loser or a winner." Not taking into account the full continuum.	_____	
Taking events out of context	After a successful interview, focusing on one or two tough questions. "I blew the interview."	_____	

Type of Error	Examples	I have had this type of thought	Example
Jumping to conclusions	"I have a swollen gland. This must be cancer."	_____	
Overgeneralizing	"I always fail— I fail at everything I ever try."	_____	
Self-blame	"I'm no good." Blaming total self rather than specific behaviors that can be changed.	_____	
Magical	"Everything is bad because of my bad past deeds."	_____	
Mind reading	"Everyone there thought I was fat and ugly."	_____	
Comparing	Comparing self with someone else and ignoring all of the basic differences.	_____	
Catastrophizing	Putting the worst possible construction on events. "I know something terrible happened."	_____	

What can be done about these automatic thoughts? How can they be brought under control? First of all, to become more aware of your thoughts simply count them. Counting helps you become aware of the fact that those thoughts just appear out of nowhere. They are automatic. They are not tied into reality. It is better to become aware of them than have them continue to live in the underground caves of your mind. How can you remember to count them? What can you do to keep track of them? There are several ways to accomplish this. You could use a plastic wrist-attached golf counter or a grocery store price counter. Some people use money to keep track. They keep a good supply of change on hand and transfer pennies and dimes from one pocket to another for each negative thought. Some keep track on a 3 x 5 card. Choose whatever system would work best for you.

Another way to become aware of your negative thoughts is to give yourself a goal of collecting negative thoughts. Set aside a half hour and tell yourself "This is the time for negative thought collection." Think back over the day and write down the negative thoughts which you experienced. You may want to limit the thoughts to a specific situation such as an event or interaction with a particular person.

But this sounds like work! You are so right. And if you are like most people there will be a tendency to delay and create some excuse to put off becoming a collection agent. "This is so different," "I'll do it later," "I don't like looking at my negative thoughts," and "I don't have what I need to count them at this time" are all variations of the same theme. In order to eliminate habits and change thought patterns it will take sincere concentrated effort over a period of time. Change always involves cost. If you don't like what is happening in your life, why keep on doing it? There is a better way.

If you are like most people you may have a tendency to blame yourself for these negative thoughts. Please do not! Because they are automatic they are simply reflecting a well-established habit pattern or depression. Your only job is to become aware of them. You will probably begin to think that you are now having more negative thoughts than before. However, it is just that you are now more aware of them. Your ability to catch them is improving. Eventually counting them begins to decrease them.

Remember that these automatic thoughts are reflections of some inner feelings. When the thoughts come in, try to get in touch with your feelings. Doing this can help you recapture the thought if you had difficulty remembering it.

The second major step in eliminating automatic thoughts is learning to answer them. But this cannot be done unless you catch them and identify them. The key point to remember in answering them is that there are DIFFERENT INTERPRETATIONS OF EACH SITUATION. Some interpretations are closer to the truth than others. Therefore, your task is to develop as many additional possible interpretations as possible. Often we confuse our thoughts with facts even when the two do not necessarily relate. Questioning your negative and automatic thoughts will help you create a new form of thinking.

Here is a list of twenty questions which can be very helpful in learning this new art of challenging our thoughts.

1. *What is the evidence?* Ask yourself the question, "Would this thought hold up in a court of law? Is it circumstantial evidence?" Just because your mailman misses delivering the mail one day does not mean that you cannot count on anything. Just because you tripped walking into your new class and everyone laughed does not mean that you will trip again or that they think you are a clod.

2. *Am I making a mistake in assuming what causes what?* It is often difficult to determine causes. Many people worry about their weight and if they gain weight they make the assumption that "I don't have any will-power." But is that the only reason? Could there be other causes such as glandular inbalance, using eating as a means to deal with unhappiness, etc.? We do not know the causes of obesity for certain. The medical profession is still studying the problem.

3. *Am I confusing a thought with a fact?* Do you say "I've always failed before so why should this be any different?" Calling yourself a failure and then believing your name calling does not mean the label you've given yourself is accurate. Check out the facts with yourself and with others.

4. *Am I close enough to the situation to really*

know what is happening? You may have the thought "The management of my company does not like my work and they are probably planning on getting rid of me in the next three months." How do you know what management is thinking? Are you on the management level? Is your assumption correct? Is your source of information accurate? How can you determine the facts?

5. *Am I thinking in all-or-none-terms?* Many people see life as black or white. The world is either great or lousy. People are either all good or all bad. All people are to be feared. Again where did you get this idea? What are the facts?

6. *Am I using ultimatum words in my thinking?* "I must *always* be on time or no one will like me." That is an unfair statement to make about yourself or anyone else. Notice the following example of how our words can create problems. It is the inner conversation of a woman whose boyfriend left her for another woman. This woman was attending college where there were numerous other men available.

Negative thoughts	Answers
He shouldn't have left me for another.	I don't like it, but he should have left because he did. For all the reasons I don't know of, he should have left. I don't have to like it, just accept it.
I need him.	I want him back, but I don't need him. I need food, water, and shelter to survive. I don't need a man to survive. Thinking in "needs" makes me vulnerable.

Negative Thoughts	Answers
This always happens to me, and it will never change.	Just because it happened in one case doesn't mean it has happened or will happen in every case.
This is terrible, awful, horrible.	These are labels I add to the facts. The labels don't change anything and they make me feel worse.
I must have someone to love me.	It's nice to love and be loved, but making it a condition to be happy is a way of putting myself down.
I'm too ugly and too fat to find anyone else.	"Too" is a relative concept, not some absolute standard. Thinking like this is self-defeating and stops me from trying.
I can't stand being alone.	I can stand difficulties—as I have in the past. I just don't like them.
I made a fool out of myself.	There's no such thing as a fool. Foolishness is only an abstraction, not something that exists. This mislabeling doesn't do me any good and makes me feel bad.
He made me depressed.	No one can make me feel depressed. I make myself depressed by the way I'm thinking.[2]

7. *Am I taking examples out of context?* A woman overheard the conversation of an instructor talking to another instructor about her. She thought the instructor said she was rigid, pushy and dominant. Fortunately, she checked out the conversation with one of the two instructors and discovered that she had been described as having high standards and determination. The words were spoken in a positive context, but because of her tendency to think the worst, distortion occurred.

8. *Am I being honest with myself?* Am I trying to fool myself or make excuses or put the blame on others?

9. *What is the source of my information?* Are your sources accurate, reliable, trustworthy and do you hear them correctly? Do you ask them to repeat what they say and verify it?

10. *What is the probability of my thought occurring?* Perhaps your situation is so rare an occurance there is little chance of your worry coming true. One man had the thought that because he had missed work for two days he would be fired. After he thought about it he said, "Well, I've worked there for several years and have a good record. When was the last time anyone was fired where they missed two days work? When was the last time they fired anyone?"

11. *Am I assuming every situation is the same?* Just because you didn't get along at the last two jobs does not mean that you will not get along at your new one. Just because you failed algebra the first time around does not mean you will fail it the second time.

12. *Am I focusing on irrelevant factors?* Of course there are problems in the world and people are physically and mentally sick and there is crime, etc. What can you do to eliminate these problems by sitting around worrying about them or becoming depressed over them? How else could you use your thinking time in a more productive manner?

13. *Am I overlooking my strengths?* People who worry or who are depressed definitely

overlook their positive qualities. They do not treat themselves as a friend. They are hard on themselves and focus upon their supposed defects instead of identifying their strengths and praising God for them. It is important not only to list your strengths but also recall times in your past when you were successful.

14. *What do I want?* This is a question I ask people over and over again in counseling. What goals have you set for your life? For your worry? What do you want out of life? How do you want your life to be different? What is the fear that you want to be free from at this point in your life?

15. *How would I approach this situation if I were not worrying about it?* Would I tend to make it worse than it is? Would I be as immobilized by the problem as I am now? Imagine how you would respond if you believed that you had the capabilities of handling it.

16. *What can I do to solve the situation?* Are my thoughts leading to a solution of this problem or making it worse? Have I written down a solution to the problem? When was the last time I tried a different approach to the problem?

17. *Am I asking myself questions that have no answers?* Questions like "How can I undo the past?" "Why did that have to happen?" "Why can't people be more sensitive?" or "Why did this happen to me?" Often questions like these can be answered with the question "Why not?" What if something terrible happens? "So what if it does?" Why spend time asking yourself unanswerable questions.

18. *What are the distortions in my own think-*

ing? The first step in overcoming errors is to identify them. Do you make assumptions or jump to conclusions? What are they? The best way to deal with an assumption is to check it out. Look for the facts.

19. *What are the advantages and disadvantages of thinking this way?* What are the advantages of worrying? List them out on a piece of paper. What are the advantages of thinking that people don't like you? What is the benefit of *any* type of negative thinking?

20. *What difference will this make in a week, a year, or ten years?* Will you remember what happened in the future? Five years from now who will remember that your shirt was buttoned wrong? Who really cares? We believe that our mistakes are more important to other people than they really are. If someone chooses to remember ten years from now, something you said or did that bothered them, that's their problem, not yours.[3]

To create new interpretations, write down all possible interpretations. List as many as possible, both automatic and conscious thoughts. "What if I fail that exam?" or "I will fail that exam because I am dumb." Challenge each thought and write down new interpretations. Then act on your new interpretations if action is needed.

All of this can be a practical application of Philippians 4:6-9. But this passage has even more to say. It isn't a matter of just stopping, without replacing this action with a positive substitute. If a person who has been accustomed to worrying stops but does not fill that void with something else he will revert back to his practice of worrying. People cannot exist in a vacuum. They must be doing something.

Earlier you read how to identify and reinterpret your thoughts. But there is more. Paul suggests something simple. He says that in everything with prayer and supplication with thanksgiving your requests should be made known to God. There is not limit to what we can pray about. The most insignificant concern can be brought to God and He will respond. We can pray for forgiveness for the past, for what we need in the present, and for help and guidance for the future. Take your past, present, and future with all your shame, your needs, and your fears into the presence of God. And do it with thanksgiving. You might even include thanks for the actual privilege of prayer. We can give thanks in time of laughter or tears, in times of distress and pain as well as experiences of joy and delight.

There is a positive result to this practice of prayer. You will be given peace in your heart and mind. God's peace, like a sentinel or guard, will replace the worry and assist in keeping future worries away. This peace surpasses all human thought or understanding. It does not mean that this peace is such a mystery that man's mind cannot understand it—although that is partly true. It does mean that the peace of God is so complete and valuable that man's mind, with all its skill and its knowledge and all its understanding can never construct it on its own or discover it or produce it. It is another one of the wonderful gifts from God.

The passage in Philippians can be divided into three basic stages. We are given the *premise* —do not worry. We are told what to *practice*— prayer. And then we are given the *promise*— peace. It is there—available—but we must follow the first two steps in order for the third to occur. The principle of these verses is: Stop worrying, start praying, and begin receiving God's peace which replaces the worry.

A friend of mine, Dr. Jerry Schmidt, who is a Christian psychologist, shared what he does with prayer. "In a most exciting book entitled *The Edge of Adventure*, I came across what has been for me a Godsend in my own prayer life. In the book the authors outline 'Seven minutes of time with God.' In the first thirty seconds you just try to relax. Take a deep breath, and realize that God, who loves you deeply, is there with you. Ask Him to calm your heart and make you receptive to His will. During the next four minutes, you read in the Gospel of John not for factual information but with two questions in mind:

1. What kind of personality does God—the One to whom I have given my life—have?
2. Is there anything here that speaks to me for today, now?

During the last two-and-a-half minutes— prayer. They suggest the following order:

1. Adoration. Just tell Christ that you love Him—in your own words. . . . "I love you, Christ. I want to respond to You with my whole life." A line from a Psalm may be another way to do this. Any expression of

praise that comes from the depths of your soul seems to help.

2. Confession. What I do here is to lay out to God very specific things that I am genuinely sorry for. I am very specific about what I'm asking forgiveness for.

3. Thanksgiving. Again, be specific. This can be a beautiful time of searching for a discovering of all the blessings in my own life.

4. Supplication. First I pray for others and their needs. And when I get to my own needs I have often prayed ''And as for me, Lord, Thy will be done.'' This simple statement, along with the adoration part of my prayer time has helped me in letting go of my own anxiety and fears.

I often have my prayer time while I am beginning my day, jogging and exercising. That puts some real energy into it!''[4]

The results of prayer as a substitute for worry can be vividly seen in two Old Testament passages. In Psalms 34 (RSV) David, who was undergoing a crisis in his own life, begins: ''I will bless the Lord at all times; his praise shall continually be in my mouth.'' David has just escaped from the Philistines who had captured him. He had faked the role of a madman knowing that they would release him rather than kill him. He then fled and hid in the cave of Adullam along with four hundred men who are described as men who were in distress, discontented, and in debt. In the midst of all this David wrote this psalm of praise. He did not say he would sometimes praise the Lord, but would do so at all times. No exception! This must have been a fearful time for David, knowing that the enemy was still after him.

In verse four he says, "I sought the Lord and he answered me, and delivered me from all my fears." David had neither fear, worry, nor anxiety. He prayed and gave the problem over to God, who lifted it away. Nor did David turn around and take these cares back after he had deposited them with the Lord. He gave them up. Too many people give their burdens to God with a rubber band attached. As soon as they stop praying the problems bounce back. Some people pray, "Give us this day our daily bread," and then when they are through praying begin to worry where their next meal is going to come from.

Another factor to remember here is that God did not take David away from his problem. He was still in the cave with four hundred disgruntled men and he was still hiding. God does not always take us out of a problem situation but he gives us the peace that we are seeking as we proceed through that experience. It happened to David and it happens today for those who pray, unload their cares on God, and leave them there.

There are so many occasions when you and I would like to change our circumstances. Joyce and I are the parents of a fifteen-year-old son. But we do not know what it is like to be the parents of an adolescent son. Matthew is a severely mentally retarded boy. If I could change circumstances, I would want Matthew to be a normal boy so that he could experience the joys of a father-son relationship. But Matthew's condition is not going to change.

Sometimes we can understand the power and the authority of God, but we might question His wisdom in allowing this trial or that one to come into our lives. God does not reject us for that questioning. He wants us to tell Him about it. He knows how we feel anyway—we might as well tell Him. But after telling Him, let's go against our feelings in order to go to the Scripture and to affirm that God is faithful and loving and wise. He really does know what is best for us; He really is in control. Accept that, and you can be sure that even if you don't understand, He is working.

Through the experience of having a retarded son, my wife and I have learned to thank God for things we had taken for granted. We have learned to praise Him and to thank Him for His faithfulness and for the emotional stability and patience He has given us. He helps us have a sensitivity to Matthew's actions and gestures so that he can communicate with us in these small ways. In the very midst of what many people would call a tragedy, we learn to rejoice because we see God working in our lives.

You and I have many questions that will never be answered in our life. We do not have to have all of the answers for "why" something happened. I would like my boy's body and mind to be whole, but it won't happen in this life. In the resurrection, though, he will be made whole. That is the hope every believer can look forward to. The assurance of our future joy in God's presence can console us in the midst of the tragedies of this life.

God has acted before throughout history and He acts today. David learned to rejoice, to pray, and to rest in God. How is this possible for us today? The answer is in the Scriptures that have been discussed earlier. But they must be practiced and acted upon.

Both worry and anxiety are often panic reactions. The opposite of worry is faith, and someone has suggested that faith is a refusal to panic. But in order to overcome your worry with faith you have to activate your faith or put it into motion. In Luke 8:22-25 we find a situation where Jesus asked his disciples, Where is your faith? It is almost as though He were saying, ''I know you have faith but where is it at this moment?'' Faith has to be put into motion. Martyn Lloyd-Jones in his book *Spiritual Depression* suggests a way.

Faith is not something that acts automatically, faith is not something that acts magically. This, I think, is the blunder of which we have all, at some time or another, been guilty. We seem to think that faith is something that acts automatically. Many people, it seems to me, conceive of faith as if it were something similar to those thermostats which you have in connection with a heating apparatus, you set your thermostat at a given level, you want to maintain the temperature at a certain point and it acts automatically. If the temperature is tending to rise above that, the thermostat comes into operation and brings it down; if you use your hot water and the temperature is lowered, the thermostat

comes into operation and sends it up, etc.
You do not have to do anything about it, the
thermostat acts automatically and it brings
the temperature back to the desired level
automatically. Now there are many people
who seem to think that faith acts like that.
They assume that it does not matter what
happens to them, that faith will operate and
all will be well. Faith, however, is not
something that acts magically or automatically. If it did, these men would never
have been in trouble, faith would have come
into operation and they would have been
calm and quiet and all would have been well.
But faith is not like that and those are utter
fallacies with respect to it. What is faith? Let
us look at it positively. The principle taught
is that faith is an activity, it is something
that has to be exercised. It does not come into
operation itself, you and I have to put it into
operation. It is a form of activity.[5]

When you find yourself in a difficult position
the first thing to do is to refuse to allow yourself
to be controlled by the situation or circumstances. Do not panic and do not look at just the
problems facing you. The next step is to then
remind yourself of what you believe and what
you know to be true.

Your faith must be based upon the facts of
Scripture and not your feelings. Faith holds onto truth and reasons from what it knows to be
fact. That is the way faith acts but it must be
exercised.

How do you put faith into action? Samuel

Shoemaker suggests six steps which help in living a faith-filled life.

Exposure	Experience
Explanation	Expression
Experiment	Expansion

Exposure is a critical step. In order to acquire or expand your faith you need to come in contact with that which helps build your faith. Experiencing the reality of a worship experience in church, studying and meditating upon the Scripture and hearing the testimony of others who have faith gives you an exposure.

Explanation can come through classes, commentaries and practical teaching which clarifies questions and doubts.

The third step is to experiment with what you have been learning in the first two steps. Put into practice what you have received.

The fourth step arrives when you begin to experience spiritual benefits. It can also involve some type of spiritual experience in a meeting, retreat or individual prayer time.

The fifth step involves giving expression to your faith, your beliefs and the new life that you are experiencing.

The last step is allowing the love of God to expand more and more each day, letting Him direct your total life.

In order to live a life of faith and to overcome worry and anxiety you must focus upon and practice the definite promises of Scripture. When tempted to fear or worry, consider what Isaiah expressed for us:

Fear not, for I am with you, be not dismayed, for I am your God; I will strengthen you, I will help you, I will uphold you with my victorious right hand (Isaiah 41:10 RSV).But now thus says the Lord, he who created you, O Jacob, he who formed you, O Israel: "Fear not, for I have redeemed you; I have called you by name, you are mine. When you pass through the waters I will be with you; and through the rivers, they shall not overwhelm you; when you walk through the fire you shall not be burned, and the flame shall not consume you. For I am the Lord your God . . . (Isaiah 43:1-3 RSV).

Worry and tension, or calmness and peace—it's your choice.

Notes For Chapter 6

[1]Gary Emery. A New Beginning: *How You Can Change Your Thoughts Through Cognitive Therapy.* (Simon and Schuster, N.Y.), 1981. Pg. 541.
[2]Ibid. Pg. 61.
[3]Ibid. Adapted.
[4]Dr. Jerry Schmidt, *You Can Help Yourself*, (Harvest House, Eugene, OR) 1978. Pg. 112.
[5]Dr. Martyn Lloyd-Jones, *Spiritual Depression*, (William B. Eerdmans, Grand Rapids, Mich.), 1965. Pg. 142-143.

7

How to Control Your Thoughts

Thought stopping is a very helpful procedure to use to help you overcome fear. In the late 1950s, it was used by many therapists for the treatment of obsessive and phobic thoughts. Obsessions are repetitive and intrusive trains of thought that are unrealistic, unproductive and often anxiety provoking. An obsessive person is often called a "worry wart." Obsessions may take the form of self-doubt: "I will never be able to do this job right" or "I'm too plain to get a date." Obsessions may also take the form of fear: "I wonder if something is wrong with my heart" or "If they raise the rent, I'll have to move."

Thought stopping involves concentrating on the unwanted thoughts and, after a short time, suddenly stopping and emptying your mind. The command "Stop" or a loud noise is generally used to interrupt the unpleasant thoughts. There are three explanations for the success of thought stopping: 1. The command "Stop" serves as a punishment, and behavior which is consistently punished is likely to be inhibited; 2. The command "Stop" acts as a distraction which is incompatible with obsessive or phobic thoughts; 3. Thought stopping is an assertive response and needs to be followed by positive thought substitutions of reassuring or self-accepting statements. For example, you say, "These big 747s are awfully safe" instead of "Look at that wing shake, I bet it's ready to come off." This is where the use of positive passages from God's Word can be so helpful.

It has been well established that negative and frightening thoughts invariably create negative and frightening emotions. If your thoughts can be controlled, your overall stress level can be significantly reduced. For this to be effective, thought stopping must be practiced conscientiously throughout the day for three days to one week with consistency.

The first step is to explore and list your stressful thoughts. Use the following stressful thoughts inventory[1] to help you assess which recurrent thoughts are the most painful and intrusive.

STRESSFUL THOUGHTS INVENTORY
Put a check mark after each item that applies to you. For items which you check, rate them in column A from 1 to 5, based on these statements:
1. *Sensible.* This is quite a sensible and reasonable thing for me to think.
2. *Habit.* This is just a habit. I think it

automatically without really worrying about it.

3. *Not Necessary.* I often realize that this thought is not really necessary, but I don't try to stop it.

4. *Try to Stop.* I know this thought is not necessary. It bothers me, and I try to stop it.

5. *Try Very Hard to Stop.* This thought upsets me a great deal, and I try very hard to stop it.

For items which you check, rate them in column B from 1 to 4, based on the following statements:

1. *No Interference.* This thought does not interfere with other activities.

2. *Interferes a Little.* This thought interferes a little with other activities, or wastes a little of my time.

3. *Interferes Moderately.* This thought interferes with other activities, or wastes some of my time.

4. *Interferes a Great Deal.* This thought stops me from doing a lot of things, and wastes a lot of time everyday.

	Check here if your answer is yes	A If yes, rate from 1 to 5	B R a t e from 1 to 4
Do you worry about being on time?			
Do you worry about leaving the lights or the gas on, or whether the doors are locked?			

	Check here if your answer is yes	A If yes, rate from 1 to 5	B R a t e from 1 to 4
Do you worry about your personal belongings?	_____	_____	_____
Do you worry about always keeping the house clean and tidy?	_____	_____	_____
Do you worry about keeping things in their right place?	_____	_____	_____
Do you worry about your physical health?	_____	_____	_____
Do you worry about doing things in their right order?	_____	_____	_____
Do you ever have to count things several times or go through numbers in your mind?	_____	_____	_____
Are you a person who often has a guilty conscience over quite ordinary things?	_____	_____	_____
Do unpleasant or frightening thoughts or words ever keep going over and over in your mind?	_____	_____	_____
Have you ever been troubled by certain thoughts of harming yourself or others —thoughts which come and go without any particular reason?	_____	_____	_____
Do you worry about household things that might chip or splinter if they were to be knocked over or broken?	_____	_____	_____
Do you ever have persistent ideas that someone you know might be having an accident or that something might have happened to them?	_____	_____	_____

	Check here if your answer is yes	A If yes, rate from 1 to 5	B R a t e from 1 to 4
Are you preoccupied with the fear of being raped or assaulted?..............	_____	_____	_____
Do you go back and think about a task you have already completed, wondering how you could have done it better?	_____	_____	_____
Do you find yourself concerned with germs?	_____	_____	_____
Do you have to turn things over and over in your mind before being able to decide what to do?.............	_____	_____	_____
Do you ask yourself questions or have doubts about a lot of things that you do?	_____	_____	_____
Are there any particular things that you try to keep away from or that you avoid doing, because you know that you would be upset by them?.........	_____	_____	_____
Do you worry about money a lot?..................	_____	_____	_____
Do you frequently think that things will not get better and may, in fact, get worse?	_____	_____	_____
Do you become preoccupied with angry or irritated thoughts when people don't do things carefully or correctly?	_____	_____	_____
Do you ruminate about details?................	_____	_____	_____
Do guilt-tinged memories return to you over and over? .	_____	_____	_____
Do you have recurring feelings of jealousy, or fear of being abandoned?........	_____	_____	_____

	Check here if your answer is yes	A If yes, rate from 1 to 5	B Rate from 1 to 4
Do you feel nervous about heights?			
Are you at times preoccupied with desire for things you cannot have?			
Do you worry about auto accidents?			
Do you find yourself returning to thoughts about your faults?			
Do you worry about growing old?			
Do you feel nervous when thinking about being alone?			
Do you worry about dirt and/or dirty things?			
Do you tend to worry a bit about personal cleanliness or tidiness?			
Does a negative feature of your appearance or make-up preoccupy you at times?			
Do you feel that God does not accept you?			
Do you feel that you have committed the unpardonable sin?			
Do you worry about getting trapped in crowds, on bridges, elevators, etc?			
Do you think again and again about your failures?			
Sometimes do you think about your home burning?			
Do you think frequently of certain things of which you are ashamed?			
Are you preoccupied with uncomfortable thoughts about sex or sexual adequacy?			
Do you worry about God being angry at you?			

Ask yourself these questions about each stressful thought you checked: Is the thought realistic or unrealistic? Give two examples

_____

Is the thought productive or counterproductive? Give two examples _____

_____

Is the thought neutral or self-defeating? Give two examples _____

_____

Is the thought easy or hard to control? Give two examples _____

_____

Thought stopping requires consistent effort. List your specific reasons for stopping any of the thoughts you have selected. _____

_____

Select now a thought that you feel you really want to eliminate. Column A is the discomfort rating for each thought, while column B is the interference rating for how disruptive it is to your life. Any thought that has a discomfort rating above three, or an interference rating above two may warrant thought stopping procedures.

Now close your eyes and imagine a situation in which the stressful thought is likely to occur. Try to include normal thoughts as well as obsessive thoughts. In this way, you can interrupt the stressful thoughts while allowing a continuing flow of healthy thinking.

THOUGHT INTERRUPTION

Thought interruption can be accomplished by using one of two "shock" techniques:

Set an egg timer or alarm for three minutes. Look away, close your eyes, and think about your stressful thought. When you hear the ring, shout "Stop!" Do this out loud and do it twice. You may also want to raise your hand or snap your fingers or stand up. Let your mind empty of all but the neutral and nonanxious thoughts. Set a goal of about thirty seconds after the stop, during which your mind remains blank. If the upsetting thought returns during that time, shout, "Stop!" again twice.

Another approach is to write the word "stop" on a 3 x 5 card with Philippians 4:6-9.

Your next step is to take control of the thought stopping cue, but without the timer or tape recorder. While thinking about the unwanted thought, shout "Stop!"

When you succeed in eliminating the thought on repeated attempts with the shouted command, begin countering the thought with "Stop" said in a normal voice.

After you succeed in stopping the thought by using your normal speaking voice, attempt to do the same with a whisper.

When the whisper is sufficient to stop your fearful thoughts, use the command "Stop" in your mind. Imagine shouting "Stop!" in your mind. Success at this point means that you can stop thoughts at any time and in all situations.

THOUGHT SUBSTITUTION

The last phase of thought stopping involves thought substitution. In place of the obsessive thought, make up some positive, assertive statements that are appropriate in the target situation. For example, if you are afraid of flying, you might say to yourself, "This is a fantastically beautiful view from way up here." Develop several alternative assertive statements to say to yourself, since the same response may lose its power through repetition.

THOUGHT SWITCHING

When you think, imagine, daydream or fantasize, you often give yourself a set of instructions that ensures your acting in a fearful manner. These instructions soon become habits. One of the best ways to break a habit is by setting up a more powerful counterhabit. Here the counterhabit you are trying to achieve is that of teaching yourself not to be fearful. With Thought Switching you do not try to stop your worrisome thoughts of doom directly as you do with Thought Stoppage. Instead you (1) select a series of counterthoughts and (2) deliberately strengthen these thoughts until they become strong enough to override or replace the anxiety thoughts. This exercise is adapted from a method devised by Dr. Lloyd Homme, a California psychologist.

The purpose is to replace your fear self-instructions with positive self-instructions.

STEP ONE: The first step is to recall what you usually say prior to the fear on which you are now working. List the self-instructions you give yourself (the small, detailed ones as well as the big, overwhelming ones). For example, here are the self-instructions a person who feared elevators gave himself.

1. "As I enter the building, I will start thinking about all the terrible things that can

happen to me on the elevator."

2. "When I enter the building, I will strain to see if any people will be getting on the elevator with me."

3. "I will look around to make sure there is a staircase—what if I get stuck up there and I can't get back down!"

4. "I will make myself notice whether it's an express elevator or not. I will begin to wonder what if it gets stuck in the part where there are no openings."

5. "When I'm in the elevator, I will stand near the front (or the back). I will tighten my muscles and make myself think of all the bad things that might happen."

6. "I will pay attention to the slightest sound or vibration and deliberately make myself think of them as signals that things might be going wrong."

STEP TWO: For each of these self-instructions set up a list of coping self-instructions. Your aim: to set up the opposite habit of thinking so that you will be able to handle whatever comes along. Here is the list that the elevator phobe worked out:

1. "As I enter the building, if I start thinking about the terrible things that might happen, I will tell myself that very little chance exists that anything bad will happen."

2. "If I find myself noticing whether people are getting on the elevator, I will tell myself that it really doesn't matter if other people are on the elevator."

3. "If I find myself searching for the stair-

case, I will tell myself that even if I'm nervous about coming down in the elevator, I will be able to cope with it."

4. "I will start thinking that there is very little chance of anything bad happening."

5. "When I'm on the elevator, I will deliberately relax my muscles and think about something pleasant."

6. "If I hear an unusual noise, I will tell myself that even if something goes wrong, at most it will be a minor inconvenience."

STEP THREE: Put each of the new self-instructions you have worked out for yourself on a separate card. The order doesn't matter. Carry the cards with you or stick them in a convenient place—in your purse, on top of the night table, by the telephone, etc.

STEP FOUR: Take a group of actions you perform fairly frequently every day: drinking coffee or soda, changing channels on the TV set, running a comb through your hair, washing your hands, making a phone call. Each time, just before you do one of these high-frequency acts, take your topmost card, read it carefully and say the instruction to yourself. Then take your first sip of coffee, turn the TV channel or run the comb through your hair. Alternate way: Say the new instruction before you do something that gives you pleasure—read your mail, eat cake, watch a favorite TV program.

STEP FIVE: When you're in the real life situation, deliberately repeat the instructions and try to follow them. It may take several weeks, but your anticipatory thoughts should change and your anxiety decrease.

STEP SIX: After using your self-instructions for awhile, you may think of better statements. Don't hesitate to switch, but don't change too often. You want to get enough practice with each new self-instruction so that it starts to take hold.

If you fail your first attempt at stopping a thought it may mean that you have selected a thought that is very difficult to eliminate. Try selecting an unwanted thought that is less fearful than your initial choice. It is more important to become proficient at stopping any thought before working on the more fearful thoughts.

If saying "Stop" is not successful for you, or you find it embarrassing to say "Stop" aloud in public, you can substitute one of the following: Put a rubber band around your wrist, and when anxious thoughts occur, pull back and snap it. Or pinch yourself when the thoughts happen.

Another approach which can be used to bring greater freedom from fear and a general sense of relaxation is the following tape exercise.[2] Have someone with a pleasant sounding voice tape this entire sequence following the time designations.

A TAPE FOR RELAXATION THERAPY

You are about to enter upon an experience of relaxation and meditation. There are four requirements for a good experience.

1) A quiet environment. The best location will be a spot where you will not likely be disturbed. This need not prevent the experience; you can be sitting on a bus, or in some crowded place, but it will be much more effective if you can be

in a situation where you will not be disturbed.
2) A comfortable position. Although you need a comfortable position you should not lie down because you will have a tendency to go to sleep. This is not your aim. Sleep is a different state from relaxation and not as desirable. So just make sure that you are in a place where you feel comfortable.

3) An object to dwell on. As you progress through this experience you'll be led by my voice and your attention will be taken through a series of stages. Ultimately you will be guided to focus on a statement from the Bible. Follow naturally after this leading.

4) A passive attitude. Although there will be a focal point for your thoughts it may be that your mind will wander. Don't worry about this. Remain passive. Just gently turn your mind back to my voice. You do not have to worry about your wandering mind. This is a relaxation program. Nothing about it should worry you or raise your anxiety. (20 seconds pause)

You do not need to worry about anything at this time. You are going to forget all about things that have worried you, bothered you, or upset you. (20 seconds pause)

Let it be a quiet place, perhaps by the seashore where the waves are lazily rolling up on the sand, and the cool breeze is brushing your face, or in a mountain setting where you are looking out over a beautiful valley and everything looks calm and serene, or maybe in a grassy meadow, or even in your own backyard. (20 seconds pause)

Now see yourself as actually being in your

ideal place for relaxation. On the screen of your mind you are seeing all the colors, hearing the sounds, smelling the aromas. If it is a grassy field, you feel the lush grass beneath you, the warmth of the sun shining upon you, the smell of the new-mown hay, you hear the buzz of the bees, overhead you see the fluffy white cotton-candy clouds as they drift lazily across the blue sky. Just feel yourself enjoying the soothing, quiet, refreshing environment. (20 second pause)

Feel the restfulness, the calmness of your wonderful situation, and let your whole body and mind be renewed and refreshed. (20 seconds pause)

Now focus your attention upon your breath. Breathe deeply and evenly, deeply and evenly, think of nothing but your breath as it flows in and out of your body. (20 seconds pause)

Say to yourself, I am relaxing, breathing smoothly and rhythmically, fresh oxygen flows into my body, I feel calm, renewed, and refreshed. (20 seconds pause)

The Bible says, "Be still and know that I am God" (Psalm 46:10 RSV). "Be still" literally means, "let your hands drop," "give up fighting." That is what I want you to do. Quit struggling. Leave yourself in the hands of God. You don't need to struggle. He will do it for you. From this time on we will follow a program of being still and relaxing. (20 seconds pause)

Now direct your attention to the muscles of your feet and ankles. Imagine the muscles are becoming very loose and relaxed. You can let the tension and tightness flow out of your body. (20 seconds pause)

Now let the attention focus on the calves of your legs. Imagine that they are becoming very deeply relaxed. (20 seconds pause)

Address your attention now to the muscles in your thighs. Let the muscle become deeply relaxed, just let go and let the muscles of your legs become completely relaxed. (20 seconds pause)

As your hip muscles are becoming more and more relaxed let your attention shift to the muscles in your abdomen and your lower back. Let the muscles become very relaxed, all the time breathing in peace and relaxation and breathing out tension, tightness, and anxiety.

Let your attention move to your chest muscles and the muscles in your upper back. Once again let those muscles become very relaxed. With each breath you are becoming very deeply relaxed. (20 seconds pause)

Now take time to concentrate on the muscles in your arms and shoulders. Let your shoulder muscles relax, beginning with your upper arms and descending down through each finger in your hands. You are becoming very relaxed. (20 seconds pause)

Think of your muscles as being bound with a tourniquet. The tourniquet is holding your muscles tight. Release it. Feel all your muscles go loose. (20 seconds pause)

You are now deeply relaxed—more deeply relaxed than you have been any time today. (20 seconds pause)

Take just a moment to survey the muscles of your body. If you note any place where there is tightness, let the tightness flow out of your body with your next breath. (20 seconds pause)

Concentrate upon the circulatory system of your body. See it as a pipeline carrying the life-giving blood to all the vital parts of your body. Envisage the Alaska pipeline as it comes across the snowy wastes, carrying the oil to the energy-thirsty forty-eight states. See the maintenance men guarding those pipes and their precious contents. Notice the way they work to make sure that the oil continues to flow on its way to the places where it is badly needed. Sense your blood moving through your circulatory system to every part of your body, bringing the life-giving oxygen and energy. (20 seconds pause)

Continue to focus on your breath as it flows in and out. Remember that oxygen is bringing life to your bloodstream and your heart. The Bible refers to God's Spirit as the breath of God. Feel the breath of God's Spirit entering into your body. (20 seconds pause)

We are now embarking on a program of Christian meditation. Our theme is taken from the prophecy of Isaiah, ''They that wait upon the Lord shall renew their strength; they shall mount up with wings as eagles; they shall run and not be weary; they shall walk, and not faint'' (Isaiah 40:31 RSV). (20 seconds pause)

We are now turning to a statement from the New Testament, ''I can do all things through Christ which strengtheneth me'' (Philippians 4:13). (20 second pause)

Continue to breathe deeply and evenly. As you breathe in say within yourself, ''I can do all things.''

As you breathe out repeat, "Through Christ which strengtheneth me." (20 seconds pause)

Be calm, be patient, put all your thoughts aside and concentrate on: "I can do all things through Christ which strengtheneth me." (20 seconds pause)

Don't let anything in your mind interrupt your focus on this statement: "I can do all things through Christ which strengtheneth me." (20 seconds pause)

Continue to breathe deeply and evenly. "I can do all things through Christ which strengtheneth me." (20 seconds pause)

Think again of your circulatory system. See your arteries and your veins as tubes carrying your blood to all parts of your body. See these tubes with clamps on them. The clamps are restricting the flow of the life-giving blood. Now visualize the clamps being released. Let them go—release them so your blood can flow without any restriction. The life-giving blood is flowing through your body. (20 seconds pause)

Be aware of what you are thinking, all the time conscious of accessions of strength. "I can do all things through Christ which strengtheneth me." (20 seconds pause)

Forget all the distractions that would turn your mind aside and repeat, "I can do all things through Christ which strengtheneth me."

If you feel you are becoming drowsy or your mind is racing, turn it back and repeat, "I can do all things through Christ which strentheneth me." (20 seconds pause)

Envisage your circulatory system again. See it now like irrigation channels leading all over your body. As the life-giving liquid flows across the desert, see your blood flowing into every part of your body. (20 seconds pause)

Let all your cares drop from you like some clothing you removed and dropped to the floor and recall, "I can do all things through Christ which strengtheneth me." (20 seconds pause)

Continue to breathe deeply and evenly. Deeply and evenly and repeat, "I can do all things through Christ which strengtheneth me." (20 seconds pause)

Continue to see the blood flowing freely through your body without any restriction upon it as your grow more and more relaxed. Your blood is flowing through your circulatory system. (20 seconds pause)

Now open your eyes. Rest quietly for a moment and then move into the joy of what awaits you in God's wonderful day.[2]

NOTES FOR CHAPTER 7

[1]Martha Davis, Matthew — McKay, Elizabeth Eshelmar, *The Relaxation and Stress Reduction Workbook*, (New Harbinger Publications, Richmond, CA.) 1980, Pg. 93-95. Adapted from the Leyton Scale.

[2]John Drakeford, *The Awesome Power of the Healing Thought* (Word Books, Waco, TX) Pg. 19.

8
Steps In Overcoming Fear

If you have lived with a particular fear or several fears for a long time, remember that it will take time to overcome them. In fact, you may still think you have the fear even when you have overcome it. Does this sound strange? Perhaps, but when you have lived with a fear for so long it is an adjustment to discover that a part of your life is gone.

A person who lives with a fear often learns to rely upon others in some way. To give up the fear also means giving up leaning on another person and learning to be an independent person.

Fears need to be faced gradually. It is too overwhelming to face a fear head-on in its entirety. Facing some fears all at once can be such an overwhelming experience that the fear may actually increase. The best way to begin overcoming a fear is to face it a little at a time and from a distance. A gradual approach usually works best.

Let's say you have a fear of water. Throwing yourself head first into a lake might help. But for most people the experience would be too traumatic. Wading into the water a little bit deeper each day is a much better approach.

Each year I hunt pheasants with a large black laborador that oozes energy and loves to jump upon people in its excitement. Little children (and some adults) are often frightened by these large dogs. But how they overcome their fear is a lesson for each of us. A four-year-old boy comes into the house and one of these large dogs runs up to him, tail wagging, mouth open, tongue hanging out. What does the child see? Teeth—sharp teeth, a huge black animal running up to devour him. The little boy flies to his mother, hides behind her and cries. Whenever the dog comes into the room he cries.

Then one day the boy doesn't cry but just stays behind his mother. The next day the dog is in the room and the boy comes in with his mother. They approach the dog slowly and cautiously. The dog wags its tail and looks at the pair approaching him. The child looks at the dog and its big mouth. His mother explains that the dog's mouth is open and its tongue is out because it is smiling and happy. The boy gingerly puts his hand out and pats the dog's head. The dog's tail thumps and it stretches its neck out for the boy to scratch its head. In time the boy looks into the dog's mouth and stares at its teeth. Gradually he begins to understand that the teeth and mouth are not going to bite him and eat him. How did he overcome his fear? He faced his fear right in the mouth! Not always easy—but it brings results.

As you begin to conquer your fears, be realistic about your expectations. If you were to chart your improvement on a graph, don't expect it to be a straight upward line of continuous improvement. Your growth and improvement will be a series of ups and downs and there will be times when your fears are actually worse. You need to anticipate and plan for the down times. If you don't plan for them, you will be thrown by the seeming reverse in your progress. You will begin to think that you haven't made any improvement at all. But that isn't true. What you choose to focus on at that time will affect your whole attitude for the next two days.

If you are coming to grips with a long-standing fear which you have avoided for many years, things could get worse at first. The fear can actually increase because you are coming closer to it. Overcoming fear means facing and resisting failure. If you give in to your fear it will increase.

Why don't people try the gradual approach to facing their fears? Because the idea just doesn't occur to them. They are too busy trying to avoid the object or situation that upsets them. When they do decide to tackle the problem they determine to "lick the problem once and for all" immediately. And when you think like that, the gradual approach really is foreign.

The man who finally decided to conquer his fear of driving doesn't just sit in the car for ten minutes or drive to the end of the driveway. He drives for miles and increases his anxiety making his fear worse than before. Our natural tendency is not to overcome our fears gradually.

Most of us acquire a number of problem-solving skills in our lifetime. We learn how to identify problems and how to develop, plan and execute a strategy to overcome those problems. The same procedure is necessary to overcome persistent fears or phobias. Too often we allow our fears to immobilize us and never plan a strategy to deal with them.

If you want to be successful in overcoming your fear, you will need to develop a strategy. The first step is to identify what it is you actually fear. You may think, "That is too obvious, too simple." But it isn't. If you say, "I'm afraid of people," I'm not sure what it is you are afraid of. Are you afraid of their presence, of what they say, of being rejected or attacked, of what they might think of you, or what?

If you say "I'm afraid to fly" I still do not have any idea what your fear is. Do you become fearful and anxious because of being locked up in the cabin? If so, perhaps your fear is of close places—claustrophobia. You may be frightened when you look out the window and note the height at which the plane is flying. Your fear then is more of the height. Or are you afraid of crashing?

In each situation there could be a number of aspects to fear and these must be identified. Once the identification is accomplished, then the strategy can be planned.

Take a notebook and a pen or pencil. Write down the fear or worry you have. Then list all of the different characteristics of your fear which are unique to your fear. People who are afraid of elevators may be concerned about being all by themselves, being up high, the sensation of falling, or being locked up in close quarters. They may be afraid of meeting a stranger or of being alone with a person of the opposite sex.

Some of your fears may have only one or two points whereas others may have five or six. Once you have listed your specific fears, rank them in order of importance beginning with whatever you fear most. If you are afraid of dogs and your fear increases the closer they are to you, then it is obvious your fear has to do with their proximity rather than their breed or size. Once you have ranked your fears write down the words ''Past Experiences with This Fear.'' Underneath this title describe two or three times when you actually experienced this fear because of being in the actual situation. Immediate situations are better than ancient history. Give as many details as possible of these encounters. Then compare your description with the important characteristics which you indicated earlier to see if they coincide.

Can you remember what you actually said to yourself at the time you experienced your fear? Your words under such conditions are very important because your inner statements could have reinforced your fear response. Statements may include ''I feel awful,'' ''I wish I was out of here,'' ''This is a terrible experience,'' or ''I can't handle this.''

Be as specific as possible when it comes to listing your reactions to these past fearful situations. Did you become immobilized or did you run? Did you try to remain calm and confront your fear or did you scream and run away? What

did you feel when you last confronted your fear?
Did your heart beat faster? Did you perspire?
Did you feel like fainting or did your stomach
begin grinding? List all of your physical symptoms the last time you met your fear face to
face. Here is a sample chart that you can use for
this process.

1. What I feared _____
2. The important characteristics of what I
    feared.
    A.

    B.

    C.

    D.

    E.

    F.

    G.

    H.

3. My past experience with this fear

4. My reactions

    A. What I said

    B. What I Did

C. What I felt

5. How fearful was I?

1   2   3   4   5   6   7   8   9   10

You will notice that we have now added a scale from 1 to 10. This scale is to help you assess your level of fear or anxiety when you come face to face with your fear. Circle the number which best represents how you feel in the fearful situation listed above. A (1) means there is little or no fear, (5) means a moderate amount of fear, and (9) or (10) means you were greatly upset.

What Is Your Plan?

Regardless of what you fear you need a plan to help you begin to overcome your fear. You have just completed the initial step in overcoming your fear—you identified it in specific terms. Your next task is to plan a strategy that you can use to approach your fear in a gradual manner in order to master it. In order to accomplish this you will need to use visual imagery which enables you in your mind to approach the object, situation or person you fear. You will begin imagining the least threatening situation and gradually move to the most threatening, each scene building upon the previous one. In other words, you are building a fear hierarchy.

Perhaps you are feeling that this is not what you expected when you picked up this book. Not only does this sound ridiculous and foreign to you, it sounds like a lot of work. Perhaps, but what methods have you tried on your own and what has been the outcome? What do you have to lose by continuing on? Look at all you have to gain if it works. You may be afraid that by following this procedure you may actually experience some fear and anxiety. However, if you follow the specific guideline given, your anxiety should be minimal when you mentally rehearse the situation. Here is a list of two different hierarchies[1] which will give you a better idea how to do your imagining.

SAMPLE HIERARCHY FOR FEAR OF FLYING IN AIRPLANES

1. I look at an advertisement for an airplane flight to Europe.
2. I look at color pictures of airplanes.
3. I visit an airport and look at the planes. While I am there I see a friend or relative board a plane to go on vacation.
4. I call an airline in practice getting flight information.
5. I arrange with a local pilot to visit the airport and see a small private plane.
6. I visit the airport and see the planes. I sit inside the pilot's small plane while the engine is started. There is no attempt to fly the plane. I just get comfortable sitting in the cabin.
7. I imagine myself on a regular jet plane getting ready for takeoff. The details for this and the remaining scenes I imagine are provided by a friend or relative.
8. I imagine myself on a jet while it is in flight. I am with several friends or relatives.
9. I imagine myself on a jet while it is in flight. I am by myself.

10. I imagine myself on a jet while it is in flight. I am by myself and the ride is somewhat bumpy.
11. I imagine myself on a jet by myself and the plane is landing.
12. I take a short plane flight with a friend or relative.

SAMPLE HIERARCHY FOR FEAR OF THE DARK

1. I am in a room with a friend and the lighting is fairly dim.
2. My friend and I light two candles and I turn off all the electric lights.
3. My friend and I are in the room together and I blow out one of candles.
4. My friend and I are in the room together. My friend blows out the remaining candle and we talk to each other while the room is dark. After five seconds my friend turns on an electric light.
6. My friend and I repeat scene 5, but this time we don't talk.
7. My friend and I repeat scene 6, but this time we wait a full minute before turning on the light.
8. My friend and I repeat scene 7, but this time we wait five minutes before turning on the light.
9. I am alone in the room and the electric lighting is dim.
10. I am alone in the room and there are only two candles lit.
11. I am alone in the room and there is only one candle lit.
12. I am alone in the room and there is only

one candle lit. I call my friend on the phone, blow out the candle, and talk for a couple of minutes. Then I turn on the electric light and finish my phone conversation.

13. I am alone in the room and there is one candle lit. I blow it out and wait five seconds before I turn on the electric light.

14. I repeat step 13, but this time I wait twenty seconds.

15. I repeat step 13, but this time I wait a full minute.

16. I repeat step 13, but this time I wait five full minutes.

Notice now how each of these hierarchies is structured. In each example it is arranged so the person starts with the least fearful scene. And remember, this is just creating the mental images, not facing the actual fear. And notice that in a hierarchy such as this the number of scenes will vary from eight to twenty depending upon how many you construct and need for your own mental exercise. The more gradual the approach you would like to build, the more scenes you include in your imagination.

In creating the scenes some people choose to create an imaginary venture whereas others prefer to actually go through a real life sequence in their mind. For some, to rehearse the ''real thing'' is too much of a threat at first so they choose to build a safer scene. That is perfectly all right.

The types of scenes you include in your hierarchy will depend on your own circumstances and fears. In your visual scenes you can include friends, relatives or whoever you feel you need to provide support and help in overcoming your fear. As you create the scene in your mind, begin with a scene that would be only a bit unsettling to you. The fear must be very small because you want to be able to eliminate that fear in your own mind and relax during this process. If your first scene in your mind creates too much fear and anxiety, back off and create one which is less stressful.

Here is an additional example. Note carefully the progression the person followed in creating this visual imagery. John was a college student who was petrified to speak in front of a class or a group at church. He wanted to be a school teacher so he knew that something had to be done to eliminate his fear. He committed himself to the program of creating this visual imagery. Here was his list.

1. I imagine myself practicing reading from a book out loud with no one else in the room or likely to walk in while I am doing this.

2. I imagine myself practicing giving a lecture out loud when no one else is home or likely to walk in.

3. I see myself tape recording myself just talking out loud. Then I listen to myself in the safety of my room and list every positive point that I can of my presentation.

4. I see myself practicing reading to my best friend out loud and he keeps giving me compliments.

5. I practice reading out loud to three friends in my room for fifteen minutes.

6. I practice giving a brief lecture on the meaning of a passage of Scripture to one of my close friends in my room. Afterwards he helps me with some suggestions and immediately I give the same presentation with the new suggestions.

7. I imagine myself giving this same presentation to several of my friends in my room. I see myself starting out a bit uptight but then I relax and pretty soon there is no tension. The presentation goes quite well and each one tells me that I did a good job and I feel good about it.

8. I imagine myself filling in for one of the teachers at church in a high school class of five students. I see myself being not too nervous. After I meet each student I give a brief devotional and they listen to me. It goes quite well.

9. I attend a college conference with my friends. During an open meeting I raise my hand and share my thoughts which I have just rehearsed in my mind. Other people are interested and attentive to me and then my friends all give me their response.

10. I continue to speak up in meetings and set a goal of speaking at least three times in each meeting.

Notice how the college student gradually built up to a very fear-provoking situation for the final scene. He did not begin with that one

because it was too threatening. As you create
your own hierarchy in your mind and on paper
don't be concerned if you have difficulty relaxing during the final scenes at first. This will
come later as you mentally rehearse the whole
process.

Now it is time for you to begin this exercise.
Use the following FEAR REDUCTION FORM
as you list your own personal fear which you
would like to eliminate from your life, then
follow the instructions.

FEAR REDUCTION FORM

First Scene — Remember this scene should be
very safe and simple with very little anxiety.

Scene 2

Scene 3

Scene 4

Scene 5

Scene 6

Scene 7

Scene 8

Scene 9

Scene 10

(etc.)

The Final Scene: This scene should be one which could make you anxious or fearful if you actually practiced it at this time.

Now go back through what you have written and add specific details to make the experience even more realistic. If the scenes that you are creating are just imaginary it is important that you see yourself as an active participant. And if the scenes you create are real life scenes you must be an active participant in them as well. Be sure you don't just "sit on the outside and observe" as these scenes are passing through your mind. Put yourself into the scene as though you were actually there.

Let's imagine you have just arrived at Niagara Falls. Close your eyes and imagine yourself at one of the viewing points. Imagine the scene as vividly as you can. Hold this image for fifteen seconds.

What was it like? Did you hear the roar of the water cascading down? Did you feel the mist blowing and the breeze in the air? What was the sky like? Were there clouds or was the sky clear? Were there other people around or were you alone? What did you feel as you viewed this spectacular sight?

Now perhaps you have the idea of what is meant by adding details. Here is another example. Remember our college student John and his concern over speaking or teaching? Here is John's revised plan with plenty of details added.

1. I am alone in my room at the dorm. Standing in the middle of the room I read out loud from a devotional book that I enjoy. I read three pages and stand up straight, use proper breathing and change my volume and tone of voice.

2. Now I use this same book as a resource but this time I give a spontaneous talk as though I were speaking to other students or a class. I imagine that the people are there and look from chair to chair as though each chair were filled. I try to feel what it would be like if there were real bodies there.

3. I now read or repeat several passages of Scripture to myself reminding me of the presence of God and the power of Jesus Christ in my life. I repeat Philippians 4:13, "I can do all things through Christ which strengtheneth me," and Jeremiah 33:3, "Call unto me and I will answer thee and shew thee great and mighty things, which thou knowest not." I visualize Jesus Christ standing with me as I speak and continue to remind myself of His very presence with me.

4. I repeat step #2 but this time I tape record my presentation and then listen to it. I make a list of what I can do to improve it and give it once again.

5. Now I am going to read out loud again. But this time my friend is there and he is sitting about six feet in front of me, very relaxed, with an encouraging smile on his face.

6. This time I am going to read again but there are three of my friends in the room sprawled about. I am still somewhat comfortable. I relax and before I begin I repeat the verses involved in step #3 concerning the presence and power of Christ.

7. Now I am back with my one friend and this time I am giving a talk without notes. I talk for several minutes in a casual way just sharing what I remember from the book. Afterwards he gives me his positive suggestions and I repeat the presentation.

8. I am at church and I walk into a classroom where I am substituting for another teacher. I introduce myself to the students and we chat for a bit. I then see myself asking a very pertinent question to get their attention. I share my devotional with them and not only are they interested but they ask some insightful questions.

9. I repeat step #3.

10. I attend the college briefing conference at Forest Home Conference grounds. I am in a group meeting of fifty students and a discussion is in progress. I raise my hand to be recognized, stand, and share my thoughts on the topic at hand. People watch, some nod in agreement and there is general interest in what I say to them.

Now take the fear that you desire to overcome and in as much detail as possible complete the next *Fear Reduction Form*.

First Scene — Remember this scene should be very safe and simple with very little anxiety.

Scene 2

Scene 3

Scene 4

Scene 5

Scene 6

Scene 7

Scene 8

Scene 9

Scene 10

The Final Scene: This scene should be one which could make you anxious or fearful if you actually practiced it at this time.

You have taken a tremendous step forward now by describing the scenes. This will help you approach your fear in a very gradual manner. But there is one more step you must take which has to do with your self-talk or inner conversations. What you say to yourself at this time may make the difference in overcoming your fear or continuing to be fear-driven. If your statements reflect negativism, you will not mature in your mastery over the fear. If John, for example, begins to say, "I'm going to forget what I wanted to say and make a jerk of myself" or "I will never learn to talk in front of people" or "This is going to be too much for me" he will hinder his progress. But if he counters each negative statement with a positive possible alternative he will relax. John could say "This is a new situation and I will learn how to handle it. I probaby won't forget what I am going to say and even if I do, so what! I can just say I have frequent lapses of memory like most geniuses." To counter the negative statement "I will never learn" he could say "That isn't true. I've learned all of my life and it may take awhile but I will get there."

Now I have one more list for you—your self-talk list. On the left side make a list of the typical negative statements you make whenever you find yourself in the situation you fear. Then on the right side list the statements you could make to yourself which will help you cope with the situation and face your fear.

SELF TALK

Past negative statements	Present and Future Positive Statements
1.	1.
2.	2.
3.	3.
4.	4.
5.	5.
6.	6.

7.   7.

8.   8.

I'm sure this sounds a bit complex and involves effort. That is true. But for many this
process has been very effective. It *is* a step in
overcoming your fear.

NOTES FOR CHAPTER EIGHT

[1]Gerald Rosen *Don't Be Afraid*, Prentice Hall, (England Cliffs,
New Jersey, 1976.) Pg. 69-71.

9

Facing Your Fear

A positive approach to overcoming fear is positive reinforcement. It is a way of learning to face situations which you fear and which you previously avoided. It involves matching up what you want to do with positive reinforcers. But you must practice this first in your imagination. At a later time you apply the same procedure in real life.

Imagine that you are afraid of heights but you want to work in a highrise office building. In your imagination you match the desired behavior (going up in the elevator to the top floor and looking out the window without anxiety) with a positive reinforcer or situation (sitting at home by a cozy fireplace with your spouse). When you are comfortable with imagining this previously fear-provoking scene, you begin to practice it in real life, but still visualizing the other positive experience. As you practice this approach you will find that your fear intensity is greatly reduced. Why? Because you are no longer avoiding the situation or reinforcing it and the danger you fear does not happen.

How long does it take for this approach to help overcome a fear? Two weeks to a month is usually required to accrue maximum benefits from this approach.

The first step is to describe the behavior you use to avoid your fear. Your avoidance behavior actually helps to create your problem. Be sure you describe it in specific terms. Here are some examples of well-defined problems that are quite common:

"I am a fifth-year college undergraduate who panics on objective tests (multiple choice, true-false, and fill-in). I know the material, but when I see the questions, my mind goes blank, my heart starts racing, my hands get cold and sweaty, and I leave the room. I want to be able to relax, concentrate, and do sufficiently well on the test to pass it."

"I am extremely anxious when I have to speak to groups larger than six people. I get tongue-tied and say what I have to say in as few words as possible. As part of my job as an engineer, I must present project proposals in a persuasive manner to the board of directors of my company. My inability to articulate my ideas in a coherent and impactful way often results in worthwhile projects getting shelved. I would like to present proposals in a persuasive enough manner that they are accepted."

"I feel too ugly and inadequate to ask out any of the girls I find attractive. When I go up to a girl to ask her out, I back off, thinking that she will say 'No.' I want to improve my self-concept and overcome my fear of rejection sufficiently so that I can date attractive women."

"My father was an alcoholic and made life miserable for everyone in the family. I grew up detesting alcohol and people who drink it. As an adult, I socialize with people who drink. I feel tense and withdrawn when I observe them loosening up and having a good time after one or two drinks. I would like to relax and enjoy talking with individuals who happen to be social drinkers."

The next step is to identify your approach behavior which is *what you want to happen*. This must be thought through very carefully and written out step by step. Ask yourself, How do I lead up to the approach behavior? What is the actual approach behavior I desire? What do I want to happen? What is the logical successful conclusion of the approach behavior? What are the surroundings for this behavior? How do I look? How do I feel? Who else is involved? What is their response to me and my approach behavior?

Let's imagine again that you have a fear of heights. Your approach behavior is being able to work comfortably in a twenty-eight story office building. The logical sequence of events would begin with you arriving at the building and walking into the building lobby. You go over to the elevator. You notice the light flicker from twenty-eight down to one. The door opens and several people walk out. You get on with some others. The elevator starts upward and you feel slightly anxious. You remember to relax and take a deep breath. You look at the people around you. Some of them smile at you or begin to talk to you. The elevator stops at several floors and people get off and get on. You stand in the elevator and watch the other people, what they are wearing, their facial expressions, hairstyles, and conversations. You feel the elevator moving up again and at the twenty-eighth floor you get off. You look around and walk casually over to the window. You look out over the city. You feel funny in the pit of your stomach for a moment and then you remember to relax and breathe deeply. You enjoy the view without further uneasiness. Your employer comes over and says hello. You chat pleasantly while you both admire the view. Then you walk to your desk and begin the day.

In order to overcome fear you need positive reinforcers. Positive reinforcers are pleasant situations or experiences that have these four qualities. 1) You can enjoy them thoroughly; 2) you can imagine them easily; 3) imagining them creates a feeling very similar to the feeling the scene would create in real life; and 4) you can easily erase the imagined scene from your mind at will.

Select three or four items from this list that give you the most pleasure:

Eating certain foods or drinking certain beverages

Watching or participating in a specific sport
Listening to or making music
Observing or being with members of the opposite sex
Engaging in your favorite hobby
Doing something you enjoy with friends or family
Reading, watching television, listening to the radio, or going to the movies
Solving problems
Being right
Being praised for something you are or do
Winning
Peace and quiet
Taking a bath or shower
Sleeping
Shopping
Being in nature
You add your own

It is important to practice visualizing positive reinforcers during a time when you are relaxed. Even though you may think it is time consuming it is an important step.

Imagine sitting at the beach in the cool surf on a warm day peacefully chatting with a friend. Fill in the details of the five senses as much as possible. Notice the feeling of the cool water on your body, the contrast of cool water and warm air, the feeling of sand on your feet, the sounds of water and your friend's voice, the smell of ocean air surrounding you, the sight of your friend sitting in the breaking surf, the sound of sea gulls. Notice all the details. See the colors and shapes of things.

You may find that you are better at imagining

in one sense than another. Perhaps the sense of hearing or touch instead of vision brings the scene more alive for you. With practice you can gradually increase the number of sensory modes through which you imagine the scene.

After you have successfully imagined the first scene, go on to some other enjoyable scenes. You choose what these are for yourself. Try to see how quickly and vividly you can bring these scenes to mind. When you have one clearly in mind, hold it for about fifteen to twenty seconds and then let it go. Relax for twenty seconds. Remember that people vary in how long it takes to bring a scene to mind. The scene should not include any people who threaten you, nor should it involve any active movement or excitement, just peacefulness. Once you have settled on a particular scene as being the most effective, stick with it. It is important to have one scene that you keep using. That scene will become a trigger to produce in you a completely relaxed state. Some other examples of calm scenes you could use include:

1. In a country meadow looking at a pond, hearing the crickets and smelling the fresh country air.
2. Walking slowly through the woods on a crisp, fall day.
3. Looking at the lights of a city from a distance.
4. Sitting in front of a fireplace. It's snowing outside and the fire warms you.

The following is a scene recorded by a person fearful of social gatherings and meeting new people.

I get into my car and start the engine. It will take me about fifteen minutes to drive to the meeting. (Positive Image) As I arrive I notice a number of cars parked on the street and in the parking lot and several people walking into the building. I notice some people I don't know walking up and I note that they probably will arrive at the door about the time I will. (Positive Image) I arrive at the door and one of the individuals already there holds the door open for me. I walk in and immediately notice how many people are already crowded in this room. (Positive Image) I look for a chair in a corner or side of the room. At first I don't see one and as I stand there searching around I begin to feel the fear and anxiety build up inside me. (Positive Image) I take a deep breath and begin to relax. I finally spot an empty chair next to three other people. I go over and sit down and immediately one of them begins to talk to me and ask me questions about myself. Some of the questions are fairly direct and personal and I'm not sure how to answer. (Positive Image) I handle my reponses all right and notice the lecture is about to begin. I want to sit closer to the front so I excuse myself and select a seat in the third row between two people I don't know. (Positive Image) The lecture begins and I find that I really enjoy the time. Before I know it, the meeting is over. As I get up to leave I notice again how many people are there. (Positive Image) I leave the room and along with others walk out to the parked cars. I feel good about the meeting, my interaction with others and myself.

Now write out in detail your own scene. When you are finished, tape record it.

An alternative to tape recording your scene is to have a friend read it to you while you relax with your eyes closed. That way, you can raise your finger to indicate that you have a clear image of the part of the scene being described, at which the reader immediately says, "Reinforce." After you have clearly imagined the reinforcer scene, erased it, and relaxed, you can raise your finger again as a signal to the reader to resume reading.

Dr. Jerry Schmidt, a Christian psychologist,

has suggested the following approach in this plan of positive reinforcement.

If you'd like to decrease your worry and anxiety about some fear, first make a list of several little scenes which are related to your fear and anxiety. For example, if you are anxious at social gatherings you might come up with a list such as this:

1. Sitting at home thinking about a party coming up three days from now.
2. Seeing the word "party" in print, while you're reading a book.
3. Watching people interact at a social gathering on television.
4. Talking with one other person.
5. Sitting with two other people you don't know very well, in your own house.
6. Asking someone else a question at a small social gathering.
7. Answering someone else's question at a party where two other people are listening in.
8. Driving to a party where there will be a large number of people.
9. Walking into a room where there are ten other people whom you don't know very well.
10. Introducing yourself to someone at a party.

Now number the list of scenes in order from the least fearful to the most. Make sure that you have as many scenes that produce lower amounts of anxiety as you do scenes which produce high amounts. The ideal would be for each of your ten scenes to be ranked so that scene #2 would produce just a bit more fear than scene #1, scene #3 just a bit more than scenes #1 and #2, etc. Just be sure that your selections are specific situations which could occur in the future.

Now begin relaxing in a quiet place where you won't be interrupted. Use "muscle relaxation" and "visual imagery" techniques to allow yourself to relax. Relax for about two or three minutes. When you feel relaxed, begin imagining the first scene on your list—the one which produces the least amount of anxiety. Picture every detail. Experience it for about twenty seconds. Don't let your mind wander. Stick with that scene for the entire twenty seconds. Now turn that scene off. Turn it off completely. Return to your "calm scene" which you used during your visual imagery portion of relaxation. Just keep switching back and forth, ten or twelve times, between your anxiety-producing scene and your calm scene. You should begin to feel the tension in your "tense" scene gradually going down.

Now take scene #2 on your list and repeat the same cycle. Continue on the scene #3. Switch back and forth between your "calm scene" and "tense scene" until you feel the tension going down as you imagine #3. Stop. The next day, practice again, beginning with scene #3 and moving through scenes #4, #5, and #6. Continue on up your hierarchy of fearful situations until you reach scene #10 and can feel relaxed while imagining this scene. You should now feel less anxiety when actually approaching the real situations related to the fear you've been working on.

If you have trouble getting through one of your steps and are still experiencing a lot of anxiety with it after ten or twelve times, pick a new scene for that step. Make your new scene such that it produces a bit more anxiety than the earlier scene, yet not as much anxiety as the scene you've thrown out. Then try the difficult scene again. It is important that you make each step gradual in your hierarchy or list. In other words, don't jump from a scene that produces a little anxiety right into a scene which produces large amounts. Small steps are the key.

Let's look at another approach to overcoming the fear. Select for your positive reinforcer an enjoyable scene that is easy to visualize. What is it? Write it down. Relax as you did before in a previous step. Listen to your approach behavior scene. Be sure to put yourself fully into the situation being described. When you hear the word "enjoyable scene" imagine this newly created scene for about ten to twenty seconds. Erase it and relax as the description of the approach behavior resumes.

How often should you do this? At least twice a day in detail. Practice every day until you can listen to the entire scene without feeling fearful.

When you feel totally relaxed with the imagined scene, rewrite and retape it, dropping out every other statement "enjoyable scene." Listen to this revised scene for a few more days, until you feel at ease with only half the original "reinforcers."

Return to the original script of your approach behavior scene and retape it leaving in every third "enjoyable scene" statement. Listen to this revised scene for a few more days, until you feel at ease with only half the original "reinforcers."

Return to the original script of your approach behavior scene and retape it leaving in every third "enjoyable scene." Practice for a couple of days with this version. Then tape a version with only one-fifth the number of "reinforcers," and use this for another two days.

As the days go on, the enjoyable scene you are using as a reinforcer may lose some of its effectiveness. If that happens, switch to one of the other enjoyable scenes you have practiced imagining. Change the time of day when you practice, and practice for shorter periods of time. If your reinforcer scene loses its effect entirely, then create a new scene.

When you feel comfortable with your practice sessions you are ready to practice in real life. As you move through the real life situations you can make use of the imagined reinforcer scenes whenever you start feeling fearful.

If you don't feel quite ready to tackle the real life experience, you might want to create a simulated experience. For example, you could go to an empty classroom and practice using your reinforcer scene whenever you feel fearful.

Your ability to listen to your approach behavior scene without anxiety should occur in time. Be sure to "over-practice" your new response to make sure that your fear does not recur.[1]

What you have read about in the past two chapters is a form of mental imaging. The process has tremendous potential. Norman Vincent Peale described it in this way:

Imaging is positive thinking carried one step further. In imaging, one does not merely think about a hoped-for goal; one "sees" or visualizes it with tremendous intensity, reinforced by prayer. Imaging is a kind of laser beam of the imagination, a shaft of mental energy in which the desired goal or outcome is pictured so vividly by the conscious mind that the unconscious mind accepts it and is activated by it. This releases powerful internal forces that can bring about astonishing changes in the life of the person who is doing the imaging.[2]

Dr. Peale in his most helpful book *Dynamic Imaging* goes on to make an additional suggestion which is the ultimate solution to overcome fear. "The last and most important suggestion I have to make is simply this: Stay close to Jesus Christ always. Commit your life to Him. He was the first to teach the power of imaging. He told His disciples, quite plainly, that what they pictured with faith would come to pass. Now, after more than nineteen centuries, scientists and psychiatrists and psychologists are at last beginning to proclaim what the faithful knew all along: He was right.

"Christ does not change; He is the same yesterday and today and forever. And the truth of His teaching doesn't change either. You can count on it, indeed. You can stake your life on it.

"The most wonderful thing that can happen to any of us is to have that most profound of all experiences—to know Jesus Christ personally. You can hear about Him all your life and never really know Him. You can believe that He lived and respect Him and honor Him as a great historical figure and still only know Him academically.

"But when at last you find Him and experience His reality, when for you He comes out of the stained-glass windows and out of history and becomes your personal Savior, then you can walk through all manner of darkness and pain and trouble and be unafraid. With Him by your side, you can have the most sublime of all dynamic images and achieve a sure victory in this life and the next."[3]

Notes For Chapter Nine

[1]Adapted from: *Thoughts and Feeling. The Art of Cognitive Stress Intervention* by Matthew McKay, Martha Davis and Patrick Fanning. (New Harbinger Publications.)

[2]Norman Vincent Peale, *Dynamic Imaging* (Fleming H. Revell, Old Tappan, N.J.) 1982, Pg. 17.

[3]Ibid, pg. 186-187.

10

The Ultimate Fear

There is one appointment in life which almost all people would like to avoid. Fear of this event strikes a chord in us and we would like to pretend it does not exist. You may be conscious of this fear, yet for the most part our conscious fears are like the tip of an iceberg. What is this ultimate fear? *Death.* But you may say, "Oh no! I'm not *that* afraid of death. I don't think about it much at all." Perhaps that is one of the indications of the intensity of our fear. We "don't think about it much!"

The older we grow, the stronger looms the reality of death. We have already or soon will face the death of some of our closest family members and friends. And we begin to think more about our own death. A major task of life is coming to grips with the fact that I will not always be around and that I could die sooner than I think or wish! Such thoughts bring a certain feeling of helplessness because death is something we cannot control.

Even as Christians, saying we have no fear of death, we still would like to avoid the process of dying. We are really brought face to face with mortality when we experience a parent with a serious illness. When the parent dies, in our time of mourning we alternate between feelings of grief and denial. When we deny the reality of death we try to turn the situation into a bad dream that will be over when we wake. Man denies death, runs from it, ignores it and represses it. Remember the story of the fear of death?

Death was walking toward a city, and a man stopped Death and asked, "What are you going to do?" Death said, "I'm going to kill 10,000 people." The man said, "That's horrible." Death said, "That's the way it is. That's what I do." So the day passed. The man met Death coming back, and he said, "You said you were going to kill 10,000 people but 70,000 were killed." Death said, "I only killed 10,000. Worry and fear killed the others."

Ernest Becker in *The Denial of Death* says, "The idea of death, the fear of it, haunts the human animal like nothing else; it is a mainspring of human activity—activity designed largely to void the fatality of death, to overcome it by denying in some way that it is the final destiny for man."[1]

Robert Burton said, "The fear of death is worse than death."

The Scriptures have much to say about death:

Psalm 116:15 (AMP): "Precious in the sight of the Lord is the death of His Saints."

Hebrews 9:27 (AMP): "And just as it is appointed for men once to die and after that the judgment.''

Revelation 21:4 (AMP): "God will wipe away every tear from their eyes and death shall be no more, neither shall there be anguish, sorrow and mourning—nor grief, nor pain anymore; for the old conditions *and* the former order of things have passed away.''

What are some of your thoughts concerning death and dying? Perhaps the content of this chapter may bring some of your deepest fears to the surface. Hopefully in doing so will come to a greater sense of peace about one of the inevitable events of life.

Answer the following questions[2] for yourself.

Questions	Yes	No
a. I have never thought of myself in a traffic or plane or some similar accident.	____	____
b. I often read obituary items in the paper.	____	____
c. I see death as involving only a temporary separation from my loved ones.	____	____
d. I think that medical science is likely to make some discoveries that will extend my lifetime twenty or thirty years.	____	____
e. I seldom think about death or dying.	____	____
f. I think capital punishment is cruel and unusual punishment.	____	____

	Yes	No
g. It's always a tragedy when someone dies.	_____	_____
h. I expect to face my own death calmly and peacefully.	_____	_____
i. Exceptional medical means (drugs, support machines, etc.) should always be used to preserve no matter what a person's mental condition.	_____	_____
j. I find it uncomfortable to think or talk about a person who has died.	_____	_____
k. I am both fascinated and frightened to think about having a relationship with someone who may be terminally ill.	_____	_____
l. If a person only has enough faith, God will always rescue him or her from the threat of death.	_____	_____

What is it you fear the most? Dying or the process of dying.

1. _____ I fear death itself more than dying.
2. _____ I fear dying more than death.
3. _____ I fear neither.
4. _____ I fear both of them.
5. _____ I dislike thinking about them.

What frightens me most about dying is:

_____Fear of Pain

_____Fear of suffering—progressive deterioration and disability

_____Fear of losing control over personal decisions

_____Fear of being alone, deserted

_____Fear of overwhelming emotional feelings
_____Fear of not knowing what is happening
_____Fear of being a burden
_____Fear of humiliation
_____Fear of not being able to finish my life projects or dream
_____Fear of punishment
_____Fear of being buried before I am dead
_____Fear of not getting adequate medical care
_____Fear of the future for my loved ones left behind
_____Fear of the unknown
_____Fear of not being truly born again
_____Other

Dying means change. We are afraid of the kinds of changes that will occur in us and what these changes will do to others. Even when we think we are prepared, we also live with the fear that we will not be able to cope with our death or that of another.

What is death? It is the permanent, irreversible cessation of vital functions of the body. But not all functions stop at the same time. It used to be that lack of heartbeat was considered final evidence of death, but now the attention has shifted from the heart to the brain for a reliable indication of when death has occurred. Joe Bayly says that death is a wound to the living.

People live much longer today than they used to live. They strive for not only the good life but the long life. In 1900 the infant mortality rate was much greater than it is today. For every 1,000 live births 100 of the infants died. In 1940 for every 1,000 live births 47 died. In 1967 for every 1,000 live births there were 22.4 infant deaths. There has also been a significant decline in the death rate of mothers at birth as well.

Why We Fear Death

Why is it that we fear death so much? Why do we deny death and shrink from even discussing it? We criticize the Victorians because of their attitude toward sex. But they were very aware of and dealt openly with death.

We fear physical pain and suffering. We fear the unknown. We fear leaving loved ones and friends. Today eighty percent of the individuals in our society die away from home or familiar surroundings. This in itself creates fear because we do not want to be alone when we die.

Cyris L. Sulzberger, in his book, *My Brother Death*, says, "Men fear death because they refuse to understand it." In order to understand death we must deal with our fears of death. In her book *Mourning Song*, Joyce Landorf says, "Here, then, is part of the answer as to why death frightens us so much. While, as a Christian, I know Christ has removed the sting of death and death can never kill me for eternity—death still exists. It is still fearfully ugly and repulsive. I probably will never be able to regard, imagine, or fantasize death as being a loving friend.

"Whenever and wherever death and dying connects with us—no matter how well we are prepared for it—it still slides and slithers into our lives and freezes us with fear. Such is the nature of death."[3]

Death separates us from familiar people, places and things. We enter into a journey in which there is no hope of a return visit. We cannot write, phone, or come back.

We are fearful because the time of death is uncertain even when we are stricken with a terminal illness. A person is apparently healthy one day and dead the next. Death can be peaceful and pleasant or violent and horribly repulsive and disfiguring.

We fear death because it is an unknown. We really don't know what it is like even with the reports of the "near death" experiences.

We are all a terminal generation. Life is terminal. From the minute we are born we are engaged in the process of dying. In middle age some people begin to realize that "time is short," others feel that "time will soon be up." In older age this realization becomes more acute. The awareness that time is short can help us evaluate what is important to us and what we want to do with the rest of our time.

Let's consider in a bit more detail some of our fears concerning death. Then we will look at a different perspective on death which may assist us with our fears.

The fear of pain is an ever present fear for most of us. If we have watched friends or relatives suffer the pain of a lingering terminal illness we equate dying with pain. If we feel pain with a small scratch it is easy to assume that dying brings with it a tremendous amount of pain. One way of dealing with pain is through the use of painkilling drugs. In using this approach, however, you may sacrifice alertness for the elimination of pain. Often the anticipation of a future pain can create as much mental anguish and pain as the physical pain itself. Is pain a problem for you at this time of your life? Have you really experienced enough pain to allow the fear of it to take the edge off of living?

Men and women have always wanted to be in control of their lives. Control gives us a sense of security. We assume and fear that dying will bring the loss of independence. We are afraid that we will not be able to continue to maintain control over our lives and personal decisions if we discover that we are dying. How much do you fear loss of control? What could you do to maintain control if you found you were dying? Answer the following questions.

When I learn that I am dying I would like to have control over _____

In order to maintain control over these areas of my life I could let the following people know

_____

Some of the other ways I could plan for maintaining control over decisions are _____

_____

Another fear is that of physical disability. With disability usually comes loss of energy and control over some bodily functions, and much more difficulty in getting around. Many people are faced with the decision of losing the function or even a portion of their body in order to remain alive. What about you? What would you be willing to give up in order to remain alive? Answer these questions.

In order to remain among the living I would be willing to give up:

_____The use of one
      arm
_____The use of both
      arms
_____The use of one leg

____The use of both
legs
____The use of arms
and legs
____The use of a vital
organ involving a
transplant
____The use of my
hearing
____The use of my
eyes
____The use of my
genital organs
____The use of my
body (paralysis)
____The use of my
speech functions

Another fear is isolation or loneliness. For some reason there are people who do not fear dying so much as dying alone. And when we see friends and relatives of a dying person begin to avoid the person, we realize that the same thing could happen to us. Why do you avoid a dying person? Probably because you do not know what to say to the person. We are uncomfortable because this individual reminds us that someday we will be there, too. Our personal death awareness becomes elevated.

If your death is not sudden you could spend your remaining days in a bed at home or in a hospital. How do you want others to respond to you? Why not tell them how? You could let your friends and relatives know that you want them around when you die. Tell them that their presence will not make you uncomfortable. Let them know that they do not have to spend time talking nor do they have to have answers for you. A student nurse who was dying of a terminal illness wrote a letter to her friends and fellow nurses who were staying away from her.

"I sense your fright and your fear enhances mine," she wrote. "Why are you afraid? I am the one who is dying! I know you feel insecure, don't know what to say, don't know what to do. But please believe me, if you care, you can't go wrong. Just admit that you care. That is really what we're searching for. We may ask for whys and wherefores, but we don't really expect answers. Don't run away . . . wait . . . all I want to know is that there will be someone to hold my hand when I need it. I am afraid. Death may get to be routine for you, but it is new to me. You may not see me as unique, but I have never died before. To me, once is pretty unique!

"You whisper about my youth, but when one is dying, is he really so young anymore? I have lots I wish we could talk about. If only we could be honest . . . admit our fears, touch one another. If you really care, would you lose so much of your valuable professionalism if you even cried with me? Just a person to person? Then, it might not be so hard to die . . . in a hospital . . with friends close by."[4]

Would you feel free to write a letter like this to your friends? If not, why not? If you are afraid of loneliness and isolation when you die, take steps to reach out to others and they will reach back to you.

One of your fears may be the loss of control

over your feelings. If the control of feelings is a current problem for you this fear is probably present. Difficulty with anger, depression, and sadness is the most common. We may fear that loss of control of these emotions may make us so unacceptable that people will avoid us. But intense feelings will be a part of the process of dying. You will cry and experience anger and depression. Accept that fact that your emotions will be intense and this may help lessen your fear.

What emotions do you think you will experience at the time of dying? _____

_____

Which emotions do you fear the most? _____

_____

What will be the best way to express your emotions? _____

Face your fear of dying. Otherwise your fear of death may limit your joy of living. Realize that your fears often express your hopes or desires. If you desire many friends you are likely to be afraid that you will not have many when you die. Talk to other people about their feelings concerning death. Ask them what they fear the most. Share your own fears with them. If you are suffering with a serious illness, talk with your physician in advance concerning his approach to helping a dying person. Share with him what your own desires are for treatment.

What can the Scripture tell you about death? Listen to the words of the Psalmist and of the Apostle Paul. Then express in writing what you have learned about the finality of life.

Psalm 23 "The Lord is my shepherd, I shall not want. He makes me lie down in green pastures; He leads me beside quiet water. He restores my soul; He guides me in the paths of righteousness for His name's sake. Even though I walk through the valley of the shadow of death, I fear no evil; for Thou art with me; Thy rod and Thy staff, they comfort me. Thou dost prepare a table before me in the presence of my enemies; Thou hast anointed my head with oil; My cup overflows. Surely goodness and lovingkindness will follow me all the days of my life, And I will dwell in the house of the Lord forever" (NASB).

Psalm 73:23-26 "Nevertheless I am continually with Thee; Thou has taken hold of my right hand. With Thy counsel Thou wilt guide me, And afterward receive me to glory. Whom have I in heaven *but Thee?* And besides Thee, I desire nothing on earth. My flesh and my heart may fail; But God is the strength of my heart and my portion forever" (NASB).

Isaiah 38:10-14 "I said, 'In the middle of my life I am to enter the gates of Sheol; I am to be deprived of the rest of my years.' I said, 'I shall not see the Lord, The Lord in the land of the living; I shall look on man no more among the inhabitants of the world. 'Like a shepherd's tent my dwelling is pulled up and removed from me; As a weaver I rolled up my life. He cuts me off from the loom; From day until night Thou dost make an end of me. 'I composed *my soul* until morning. Like a lion—so He breaks all my bones, From day until night Thou dost make an end of me. 'Like a swallow, *like* a crane, so I twitter; I moan like a dove; My eyes look wistfully to the heights; O Lord, I am oppressed, be my security' '' (NASB).

Romans 8:35-39 ''Who shall separate us from the love of Christ? Shall tribulation, or distress, or persecution, or famine, or nakedness, or peril, or sword? Just as it is written, 'For Thy sake we are being put to death all day long; We were considered as sheep to be slaughtered.' But in all these things we overwhelmingly conquer through Him who loved us. For I am convinced that neither death, nor life, nor angels, nor principalities, nor things present, nor things to come, nor powers, nor height, nor depth, nor any other created thing, shall be able to separate us from the love of God, which is in Christ Jesus our Lord'' (NASB).

I Corinthians 15:50-54 ''Now I say this, brethren, that flesh and blood cannot inherit the kingdom of God; nor does the perishable inherit the imperishable. Behold, I tell you a mystery; we shall not all sleep, but we shall all be changed, in a moment, in the twinkling of an eye, at the last trumpet; for the trumpet will sound, and the dead will be raised imperishable, and we shall be changed. For this perishable must put on the imperishable, and this mortal must put on immortality. But when this perishable will have put on the imperishable, and this mortal will have put on immortality, then will come about the saying that is written, 'DEATH IS SWALLOWED UP IN VICTORY' '' (NASB).

I Thessalonians 4:13-18 "But we do not want you to be uninformed, brethren, about those who are asleep, that you may not grieve, as do the rest who have no hope. For if we believe that Jesus died and rose again, even so God will bring with Him those who have fallen asleep in Jesus. For this we say to you by the word of the Lord, that we who are alive, and remain until the coming of the Lord, shall not precede those who have fallen asleep. For the Lord Himself will descend from heaven with a shout, with a voice of *the* archangel, and with the trumpet of God; and the dead in Christ shall rise first. Then we who are alive and remain shall be caught up together with them in the clouds to meet the Lord in the air, and thus we shall always be with the Lord. Therefore comfort one another with these words" (NASB).

Hebrews 2:14-15 "Since then the children share in flesh and blood, He Himself likewise also partook of the same, that through death He might render powerless him who had the power of death, that is, the devil; and might deliver those who through fear of death were subject to slavery all their lives" (NASB).

You and I have no choice. We will die. But we can choose how we view death. We can also decide how we want to spend our remaining years; what to do with our body upon death; what we would like our funeral to reflect to those who attend; how we want others to remember us; where we would like to die if given a choice. We can learn to talk more openly about death, to fear death less, to anticipate how we would handle a terminal illness. We can determine whether or not we would allow ourselves to be kept alive on a machine. We can draw up a will and decide whether or not to carry life insurance.

You see, our faith does not spare us from physical death nor from the loss, hurt and pain of the grief process. It does offer us a hope of completion in the presence of Jesus.

For the Christian, dying is a "homegoing." David Morley describes the journey for us so beautifully: "What a joyous moment that will be, when he will be reunited with all of his loved ones who have gone on before! When, once more, the lines of communication will be reestablished, the old voices heard again, and the deathly silence at last broken forever—no more goodbyes, no more quick slipping away of loved ones into the mysterious enigma of death.

"The most glorious anticipation of the Christian is that, at the time of death, he will come face to face with his blessed Lord, his wonderful, patient Redeemer, who all of those years continued to love him in spite of the countless times the man ignored Him and went his willful way. We will not be encountering a stranger, but the best and the most intimate friend that we have ever had. When we think of death as a time of revelation and reunion, we immediately remove its venom. We can say with the Apostle Paul, 'O death where *is* thy sting? O grave, where *is* thy victory?' " (I Corinthians 15:55).[5]

For the Christian, death is a transition, a tunnel leading from this world into the next. Perhaps the journey is a bit frightening because we leave behind the security we feel here and travel into the unknown. But the final destination will be well worth the present uncertainty.

John Powell in *The Secret of Staying In Love* presents a beautiful description of the finality of life. "This book is gratefully dedicated to Bernice. She has been a source of support in many of my previous attempts to write. She has generously contributed an excellent critical eye, a cultivated literary sense and especially a confident kind of encouragement. She did not help with the preparation of this book. On July 11 she received a better offer. She was called by the Creator and Lord of the Universe to join the celebration at the banquet of eternal life."[6]

NOTES FOR CHAPTER TEN

[1]Ernest Becker, *The Denial of Death* (The Free Press, N.Y.) 1973, pg. 215.

[2]Larry Richards and Paul Johnson, *Death and The Caring Community*, (Multnomah Press, Portland, OR), 1980. Pg. 164-165.

[3]Joyce Landorf, *Mourning Song*, (Fleming H. Revell, Old Tappan, N.J.) 1974, Pg. 26.

[4]B.M. Mount, *Death—A Part of Life* CRUX 11 (1973-1974) Pg. 5.

[5]David C. Morely, *Halfway Up The Mountain*, (Fleming H. Revell, Old Tappan, N.J.) 1979, Pg. 77, 78.

[6]John Powell, *The Secret of Staying In Love*, from the Introduction.